Praise for *The Glamour Years of Flying as a Stewardess*

"And they say nostalgia ain't what it used to be! A bit of a time travel book, I was so thrilled to be transported back to the sixties by *The Glamour Years of Flying as a Stewardess* and sneak a peek into the lives of these remarkable women. From dealing with entitled celebrities and badly behaved royalty, to stretching out the economy meals to cover a shortfall without delaying the plane's takeoff (back then, airline food was so much better than today's prepackaged, tasteless fare—air hostesses actually cooked the steaks on board!), to each one of the exotic countries the author was lucky to get to see (courtesy of layovers), the book carried me along on a wave of remembrances. Between the bumps and the grind, the glamour and the prestige, there was the one perk above all: getting to see those far-flung corners of the globe which only the elite got to visit in those 'heady' (no pun intended) days. *The Glamour Years of Flying as a Stewardess* is a wonderful slice of yesteryear, a chance to lose yourself for an hour or two, and Heddy Frosell da Ponte is just the perfect travel guide. Enjoy!"

—Chris Hammer, author of *Family Can Be Murder* (Dysorganized Crime Series)

"Imagine being almost permanently on call in the days not only before cell phones, but cordless phones, too. Imagine, too, having your weight carefully monitored by your employer (a pound over target and you could find yourself unemployed) and your appearance scrutinized so you were pretty and engaging at all hours of the day or night as you served seven-course lobster dinners at 35,000 feet. Set in the era before women's lib and the #metoo movement, *The Glamour Years of Flying as a Stewardess* offers an eye-popping glimpse into the entirely male-chauvinistic world navigated by a Pan Am air stewardess back in the Swinging Sixties. Told with a terrific sense of humor and self-deprecation, Heddy Frosell da Ponte's story draws you into a world that should not be forgotten."

—Lori Titus, author of *Hunting in Closed Spaces* (Marradith Ryder Series) and *Black Magic Women: Terrifying Tales by Scary Sisters*

"Gourmet meals, comfortable seats, celebrities, sex symbols, and world travel—a time when the jet set captured the headlines and ruled the world (at least that's the way some nostalgically remember the high-flying 1960s). So if you want to be instantly catapulted back to a time when commercial air travel was still very much a novelty, *The Glamour Years* is for you. In the book, Heddy Frosell da Ponte (love the name!) tells the story of her attempt to get into the highly competitive world of the flight attendant, back in the day when applicants were evaluated for their sex appeal, as well as their brains, charisma, and mastery of multiple languages. What follows is a wonderfully entertaining journey into the glamorous world inhabited by Heddy and her colleagues, and a hilarious look at the now-antiquated attitudes they had to put up with. Heddy's memoir fills the gap left by the one-season-only ABC drama *Pan Am* (maybe if they'd had Heddy Frosell da Ponte on the writing team, ABC would have kept the show going beyond 2011). Here is an incredibly joyous book—I'd give it six stars if it was allowed!"

—M.K. Tracy, author of *No One Else*

"What do you do when your wealthy family suddenly finds themselves poor? If you're Heddy Frosell da Ponte, you go out and find yourself a job. Not just any job. Heddy became a stewardess. Take a trip back to the heyday of flying: the 1960s, when flying wasn't just about getting from one place to another; it was an event. Told with a touch of humor and a good bit of nostalgia, *The Glamour Years of Flying as a Stewardess* is the story of Heddy's years as a 'Trolley Dolly.' But the good old days weren't always that good. There were weekly weigh-ins and standards. Only the most beautiful and poised of women were chosen to work the skies. More than a pretty face, Heddy shows the tenacity and strength it took to work for the airlines and to survive in a previously 'men-only' occupation. For all of that, this isn't your standard mile-high racy novel. What it is, is an honest look back at what it took to work in the airline industry in a pre-women's-lib world, as told by a woman who lived the story. The book is a good, entertaining read, and you will learn a few things along the way, too. I highly recommend it."

—Patricia Lee Macomber, author of *Star Quest: The Journey Begins* and *STARGATE ATLANTIS: Brimstone*

"When I picked up *The Glamour Years of Flying as a Stewardess*, I'd expected a lightweight, frothy read of hilarious anecdotes about flying Pan Am on the other side of the drinks trolley. I have to say I was not disappointed in respect of the humor, but I also got a whole lot more. What the author delivers here is an insight not only into the trials and tribulations of being a stewardess back in the 1960s (regulation weight checks, anyone?), but an incredibly personal story of determination (in a pre-lib era) to grab life with both hands and make the most of every minute of it. Heddy Frosell da Ponte's once-wealthy family lost everything at the end of the Second World War (she details this in incredible, heartbreaking style in her book *The Frosell Affair*) and were left destitute. That Heddy sought out a life of glamour and international travel is remarkable in itself, but that she involved her dear mother in that travel (cheap/free flights of airline staff were a thing even back then) is nothing short of saintly. Don't expect the more racy *Coffee, Tea or Me*. But if you need an uplift, inspiration, or just something to warm your heart, this book is definitely for you!"

—Xtina Marie, author of *Dark Musings* and *Collected Christmas Horror Shorts*

THE
GLAMOUR YEARS
OF FLYING AS A STEWARDESS

Book design by:
Arbor Services, Inc.
www.arborservices.co/

Printed in the United States of America

The Glamour Years of Flying as a Stewardess
Heddy Frosell da Ponte

1. Title 2. Author 3. Memoir

Library of Congress Control Number: 2019916618
ISBN 13: 978-0-578-59614-3

THE
GLAMOUR YEARS
OF FLYING AS A STEWARDESS

HEDDY FROSELL DA PONTE

Frosell da Ponte Publishing

Contents

Introduction

Most people don't remember the glory days of stewardessing, but Heddy Frosell da Ponte lived them. A pretty female who weighed in around 100 pounds, was less than thirty-two years old, unmarried, childless, and a speaker of multiple languages, she was the ideal candidate to be employed by Pan Am in the 1960s. Pan Am then sent her to their special stewardess school where she learned additional skills necessary for flying, such as caring for sick patients, cooking fresh food and mixing drinks, setting a perfect table, and serving up a seven-course dinner.

The differences between flying during that era and today's flights are astounding. Can you imagine a two-and-a-half-hour lobster dinner served on fine china and accompanied by caviar, fine cheeses, and baked Alaska? Sometimes dinner dishes would barely be put away before stewardesses started cracking fresh eggs to prepare breakfast. And as always, stewardesses pushed the familiar drink and snack cart up and down the aisle.

This coveted career allowed Heddy to travel the world, everywhere from Africa to Europe to Asia to South America and the Middle East. Always dressed well in a dress and heels, even when off duty, Heddy and her stewardess friends saw historical sites, went on safaris, and enjoyed exceptional entertainment that most people will never in their lives have the pleasure to see.

Preface

This book is not a memoir. It is a collection of some of my funniest and most memorable episodes in my life of flying. Some were hilarious, some problematic, some scary, but none were dull.

CHAPTER 1

20th Century Fox

Let's start with how I got here. I was born in Paris, France, with a French mother and a Swedish father. After World War II, we moved to Stockholm, Sweden, where I spent my growing-up years.

In early 1960, Pan American Airways liked to hire young Swedish girls as stewardesses because of their requirement at the time for most route services that each stewardess hired had to speak English plus one other language fluently. Finding American girls who met this requirement was difficult. In Sweden, we all were taught English in the public school starting in second grade and German a year later. I already knew French from my mother. Furthermore, since good looks were a plus, blonde Swedish girls often checked that box as well.

Men had been employed as stewards from 1928 through 1944, during the years of small-propellered aircraft and seaplanes. After that, only qualified nurses were hired. Then, by 1950 and the beginning of the jet planes and longer commercial routes, airlines reverted to exclusively hiring young female stewardesses to attract the businessmen. That rule stayed in place until the early seventies.

I had never been on an airplane before and wasn't interested in flying. After all, flying in 1960 was mainly for businessmen whose

3

companies paid the bill, and it was not financially feasible for the expense-conscious traveler. A flight at that time from New York to Paris cost the equivalent of $2,600 in 2014 dollars.

I did not want to apply, but a friend of mine talked me into going to the hotel where Pan Am was holding an employment fair. I told her I had no business applying since I didn't want to fly, but she insisted I do it with her anyway. So I promised her I would come along. She was hired, and I was told to come back the next year because I was not yet the minimum age of twenty-one.

Meanwhile, I started working for an American movie company, 20th Century Fox. First, I was hired as a receptionist because I was fast at answering the phone calls. Remember seeing old pictures of phone operators with all those cords that crisscrossed each other? You had to be fast and also watch out that all the cords didn't end up looking like a knitting project.

After that, I became an assistant to the public relations director. I enjoyed watching and editing the new movies for errors or inconsistencies, as well as organizing movie premieres that the actors and other big shots attended. One of the most memorable for me was the movie *Can-Can* with Shirley MacLaine and Frank Sinatra. When this film opened, I got to be a welcome hostess dressed in a dancing skirt, net stockings with a garter, and a wig made into the special hairdo from the film.

In the late fifties, we were still manually loading the huge film reels in our small theatre. They had to be threaded around in and out and up and down and over and under to the receiving wheel, like a snake, to and from the projector. The operator had to be careful it wouldn't "jump," get stuck, or be too tight and break off. I had to prepare the second projector wheel to be ready to start at exactly the right time to avoid an interruption between reel 1 and reel 2. Remember, this was only the beginning of cinemas. I was interested in how it all worked and asked the machinist many questions.

One day I asked if I could do it. He said I would be the first woman to try, so that made up my mind. He agreed to teach me. The work was heavy and complicated, which is why women of the sixties were assumed to not be capable of doing it, but I did it. One thing led to another, and I offered to help out when he was busy. To do that I needed to be officially state qualified and also take a written test for safety and other regulations.

When the inspector arrived, he was shocked that I had picked up a "man-only" qualification. If I could manage, though, he was happy to be the first inspector to give such a certificate to a woman.

Grand Opening of 20th Century Fox movie* Can Can *1960
(Heddy is first woman on left)

CHAPTER 2

Pan Am Interview

My friend who became a stewardess did not give up on me and wrote me letters about the special class for foreigners in Miami, where Pan Am had their own flight school. That class gave special help to all future stewardesses from different countries and languages by teaching them the technical terms used by the airlines, especially ones about the engines and safety concerns. I liked my job at 20th Century Fox, but I had made my friend a promise that I would try to be a stewardess, so I decided to apply when Pan Am returned to interview candidates.

Pan Am was looking for women ages twenty-one to thirty-two (mandatory retirement kicked in at age thirty-two), between five foot three and five foot nine, no more than 130 pounds, who were not married and did not have children. For those who got the job, weigh-ins would be done at every briefing, and we were grounded with no pay if we passed our maximum weight, which was given to each of us individually during training school. We were not allowed to have children or to marry until 1970.

The interview was terrible for my confidence and self-esteem. I had to stand alone in the middle of a half circle of the hiring team.

One after the other they threw me questions in English, Swedish, French, and German. They wanted to know how I would handle different situations and how I would behave with everyone from regular persons to dignitaries. They also asked questions about my degrees and the universities I had attended. Then I was given part of an American newspaper to translate. By that time, I don't think I would have been able to understand what it was all about, even if it had been a children's book. They decided I needed to improve my English-speaking skills.

Then, worst of all, two of the women came close to me and circled slowly around me, talking to each other as if I didn't exist. "She's on the short side." "Her hair needs another color." Then I was told to open my mouth so they could inspect my teeth. "They're not very straight; she will need some work done," they said. Wearing braces had not reached Sweden yet. Then they evaluated my nails, then how I walked. Was I applying for a modeling job? I got home feeling the ugliest, most stupid person on earth.

Strangely enough, ten days later I received a letter that read, "Welcome to Pan American World Airways." I was to report to Pan Am in time for the next class for foreigners in Miami, Florida, in eight months.

CHAPTER 3

The Crossing

Getting a visa to travel to the USA turned out to be more difficult than expected, even with the proof of employment from Pan Am.

Because I had been born in France during WWII as a Swedish citizen by my father and French by my mother, I needed the quota from both countries. It took the French over two years to find my birth certificate to verify and give me the visa. Then I had to make the Swedish quota. I didn't even want the job to begin with, but I was not going to let bureaucracy and the government simply brush me aside.

Three years later, I was finally ready to go. But Pan Am wasn't coming to hire that year, so they would not fly me over like they had with my friend. If I waited too long for them to come back, my visa might expire. Unfortunately, I also would not have the advantage of the special class for foreigners.

That was fine with me. I would take a chance that I would still be (re)hired when I got there.

I could not afford an airline or a cruise ship, so I took a cargo ship. Plus, I had about sixteen pieces of luggage and two trunks. I figured I was emigrating maybe for the rest of my life and therefore took all my belongings with me.

The captain was a wonderful old man who took me under his wing and taught me to play canasta. There was also another couple traveling as passengers on the ship, and we played canasta every night of the eight days on the ocean. We were spoiled with wonderful dinners, and I'm sure I had as much fun on that ship as in a big, fancy cruiser.

CHAPTER 4

New York, Pan American

I arrived in New York City with my green card, an expired employment letter, and nowhere to go. The visa officer suggested the WMCA for women as lodging. I left most of my luggage and trunks in storage at the port and got a room at the WMCA. For the first time in my life I encountered cockroaches and all their offspring. Welcome to America.

The next day I found a room in a "Pension for Young Ladies" on East River Drive. Yes, they still existed then, with curfew at nine p.m. and no males to set foot in the building ever.

The following day I went to the Pan Am building (now called the MetLife Building), a fifty-nine-story skyscraper at 200 Park Avenue and East 45th Street, above Grand Central Terminal in midtown Manhattan. I asked to see the flight director. At that time, I guess you could still just walk in and see somebody without an appointment and paperwork. I introduced myself and apologized for the delay due to my dual nationality, but told him I was now ready to start.

I can still remember the guy's shocked face. He told me they weren't hiring at this time, but I was welcome to come back when they were. I said I didn't need to do that because I was already hired. After calling another employee to get some help, questioning me about when, where, who, and more, they left to figure out what they should do with me. This scenario had apparently never happened before.

I guess they ultimately decided that if I was so determined and resourceful after almost three years, they had better keep me.

Since nobody would know until after the training and graduation what base I would get, whether on the East Coast or West Coast, I didn't think it was wise to take all my belongings with me down to Miami for the training. I asked if they knew a place where I could put my luggage. They looked at each other, and the director said, "Just bring it here and set it in the corner over there," without a thought to ask how much I actually had. When I came back later (I can't even remember how I got there with everything), surprise, surprise.

At that point, the director just shook his head and called for help. They piled everything along the walls, almost surrounding his desk. Luckily, he had a good-sized office. He also referred me to other aspiring stewardesses while waiting for the classes to start.

The eight of us lived in a small one-bedroom apartment near the airport while we waited to be shipped down for the next training session in Miami. We took turns sleeping in the existing four twin beds, with the other four sleeping on the floor on mattresses.

Pay for a new stewardess would be equivalent to $10,000–$12,000 a year in today's money—and we weren't even getting paid yet—so with such dire monetary conditions, we used to go to fast-food places and grab bunches of small packets of ketchup and mustard and make soup with them. The corner grocery store owner helped us out by giving us old bread and expired items he couldn't sell.

On the subject of pay, we would be paid only for time spent in the air. If we were delayed for eight hours on the ground or three hours on the plane *with* the passengers, we would get nothing for those hours. Therefore, everybody wanted to fly as much as possible, especially long flights in the air, where we would get per diem compensation for meals and overnight lodging. On local flights between New York and Atlanta, for instance, where the flight time was only about four hours but our day was sixteen hours on duty because of all the time on the ground, we would get paid only for the four hours in the air.

CHAPTER 5

Training in Miami

Finally the time came for us to fly down to the Pan American Academy in Miami, Florida, to start the five weeks of training.

Since I had lost three years by waiting for my visa as an immigrant, I was now twenty-four and had to sign a paper saying that I would not quit or marry in the next three years. They didn't want to waste money on my training if I was only going to stay a short time.

We would not get a salary until after we graduated and would have our uniforms deducted from our paychecks for several months.

We were taught how to cook fresh dishes, how to mix cocktails, how to know what wine would go with what dish, how to serve a bottle of wine with one hand, and how to give it a small twist at the end to prevent a drip.

We learned how to set the tables with white tablecloths and fold napkins in fancy shapes, including where to put the fancy salt/pepper shakers, the wine and water glasses, the fancy china, each piece of silverware, and a small vase with a fresh flower. We learned to put them exactly—and I mean exactly—at measured distances from each other.

Another part of our training was learning how to carve a large roast with a big, fancy silver-plated fork and a sharp ten-inch-long knife from a cart next to the passengers.

We became experts at dishing up everything with a spoon and fork in one hand and serving caviar (one-pound jar of Beluga) from a big, ice-filled silver bowl surrounded by eggs, onion, sour cream, and small toasts or blinis.

The seven-course meal service took a minimum of two and a half hours in first class. In the beginning no foods were frozen but were prepared by Maxim's, a famous restaurant in Paris, and ready for us to cook and/or reheat and assemble. When flying to different countries, the passengers could choose a dish from Maxim's or a specialty from the country they were flying to. We even got special china from Japan to use when serving oriental dishes.

Included with meals before the dessert was a special wooden cheese tray with six or eight whole pieces of cheeses from varied countries that we were taught to cut according to that special kind. We even served baked Alaska and crêpes Suzette flambé.

The menus were paintings by Dong Kingman with motifs from your destination. In first class, the menus were 10 X 14, and smaller for economy class.

Among the wines and champagne we served were Veuve Clicquot, La Grande Dame, and Crystal. We learned the signature Pan Am move called the "clipper dip" to serve drinks, which meant bending our knees a certain way when pouring rather than the more uncouth leaning over a passenger.

First class was served whole lobsters, foie gras, roast beef, or turkey carved to the guest's taste. Even economy class had fresh food. We grilled hundreds of lamb chops and cracked twice as many fresh eggs to make scrambled eggs for breakfast.

On some shorter flights, like to London, we had to start breakfast as soon as we finished putting away dinner. First class had a choice of how they wanted their eggs, including eggs benedict. Poaching the eggs in a metal pan full of water in the oven was our worst nightmare.

Dishing up small peas in coach was also problematic. They had the tendency to roll all over the place, even without turbulence. No one was given casseroles yet. Everything was dished up on plates and served after we gave them a tray with salad and an appetizer.

On flights six hours or longer, we offered duty-free items from a cart, including spirits, cigarettes, perfumes, Hermes scarves, and even genuine jewelry and watches.

Only in the eighties did we start with a choice of movies. These came, of course, with popcorn, drinks, ice creams, and other snacks.

As you can see, there wasn't much time for us to rest, unless the flight was a long one to Africa or Asia. We learned to gobble a whole dinner in five minutes while standing up in the galley.

An important segment of our training was learning to recognize all kinds of illnesses and what to do about them—seizures, heart attacks, how to give CPR, and even how to deliver a baby. Some airlines preferred hiring women who were already trained as nurses.

Another part of our curriculum was survival skills in case we crashed in the desert, the ocean, or Alaska. (I'm not kidding.) In a big pool we had training on how to inflate the rafts and put up the canopies after getting them down from the ceiling and through the doors. (Do NOT pull the release handle BEFORE it's out the door!) We also learned how to collect rain water and repair any holes in the raft. We learned how to handle all the equipment for all different emergencies. (Don't ever use H_2O on electrical fires!)

Our written test (no computers yet) was fifty questions long with no A, B, or C to choose from. That came many years later. We were given blank charts of each aircraft for us to fill in the exact place each piece of equipment would be found. At one time we had twelve different types of airplanes, each with their own door mechanism and different places for their extinguishers.

We had hands-on training to learn how to use all those extinguishers and how to open the different doors and windows in both normal and emergency modes, together with operation of the slides and the instructions we had to give to evacuate passengers.

Every six months after that, we had recurrent training. Each one concentrated more on one aspect of stewardessing, like questions about how you would respond to this or that situation, and hands-on training for equipment and doors, evacuation, and commands, each with a written test.

My favorite training was the mock-up where our trainers simulated unexpected situations made so real with smoke, fake fires, and even crash landings. I found these to be the most valuable because each scenario was unexpected, and we simply had to do what had to be done. We all drew a written note telling what role we were to play. We might be a passenger having a heart attack, a drunk causing trouble, a hijacker, or a stewardess who had to handle each different situation. Suddenly the mock-up venue would fill with smoke, and we couldn't see anything. The ones assigned crew member duty had to do what was required: find the source of the fire; get the right extinguisher; extinguish the flames; find the exits and evacuate passengers, including the handicapped; and so on. These drills seemed very real and helped us to react correctly and automatically, without even having to think about what to do. The evacuation commands were drilled into our brains.

I have to confess I had an extremely hard time with everything, being in an "American" class, since I had missed the special class for foreigners and no help or translation was given to me. So many names of things I had never heard before. I had to skip all the after-class parties and outings just to study with a big dictionary; no Google yet. Even the English speakers had difficulty using the right words to explain technical matters such as how a wing was defrosted.

We learned how to address royalties and dignitaries, and to recognize all the military grades.

And whenever a new vaccine came out, we had to get it so we were immune from every possible illness. Beyond what the general public got, we were vaccinated for cholera, yellow fever, malaria, typhus, and many others. Some gave us fevers; some hurt for days.

We also had to abide by a strict dress code. While on duty, we were always to wear our uniform, including a jacket, hat, and gloves, even if it was 100 degrees out. A girdle to smooth out any unseemly lumps and bumps was also standard. And when on layover, we had to appear professional, in a dress and heels. Training even included learning the feminine way to cross our legs at the ankles rather than at the knees.

No pants were allowed until several years later, even to tour old ruins in Greece or Italy. After all, this was the sixties. We carried cocktail dresses for our dinners out or in the hotels.

After those hard five weeks of training, we were all relieved and excited when the big graduation day came.

And what a disappointment when we were told our greatly awaited paycheck, all of $375, had to wait because the pilots had gone on strike. We weren't officially hired yet.

The ones like me who were based in New York left Miami, and three or four of us rented a cheap apartment together near the airport.

My luck. I was unemployed the first day of my employment.

CHAPTER 6

On Call—The Beginning Life as a Stewardess

The first three years of a stewardess were spent on reserve, what we called being "on call." We had to hang around and wait for briefing to call us if/when another stewardess dropped a trip due to a conflict of schedule or sickness—usually a trip that nobody wanted.

Once in a while, though, you could get a great trip. I did on my very first call. But you never knew, so you had no idea what to pack ahead of time and needed to be ready with clothes for any country and season. A ten-day trip to Africa or Asia required light clothing and a bikini. While a seven-day trip to South America or South Africa with reversed seasons required heavy sweaters, a coat, and boots. So you sat by the phone surrounded by a bunch of winter clothes all spread out on a couch and a bunch of summer clothes spread out on another couch or floor.

If you were called, you had ninety minutes to be packed and get yourself to the gate. Never mind if it was rush hour or you encountered an accident, road closing, or blizzard. You had to be there. That's why we sometimes had to rent a commuter place near the airport if we lived too far away.

Way back when I started, cell phones or even cordless phones were not invented yet, so we literally had to sit by the phone because scheduling allowed you only three rings to answer or you were in all kinds of trouble, just short of getting fired. Three misses and you did get fired. Pan American was serious business.

We spent all our on-call time half dressed in uniform 24/7 (they loved to call us at three a.m.) for a whole month, six times a year, for three years. We even had to call scheduling for permission to go to the bathroom or shower (ten minutes only). After a couple of days of waiting, you sometimes got bold and took a chance to leave your post even though you knew for sure it would be the exact time scheduling would call. Today's flight attendants cannot imagine how lucky they are to be able to live an (almost) normal life and to move around with their cell phones when they're on call.

The last day of your standby, when you started slowly to relax, thinking in half hour you would be soaking in the bathtub and getting a good night's sleep, that very last half hour seemed to always be the time the call would come. You would be so exhausted from sleep deprivation and from doing nothing for sometimes thirty days that you would arrive at your assignment a total basket case. The aircraft door would slam behind you and passengers stare at you as you walked all the way to the back as if you were late for the flight. All the storage spots would be taken by then, so you would have to throw your luggage in the restroom until after takeoff when you could rearrange some other place for your carry-on bags.

If you could survive three years of this, you could survive anything, or else you quit.

CHAPTER 7

Seniority

The goal of reaching seniority ruled our lives. We couldn't wait to gain some years. Without it we never had a chance of getting the best layover or the days off we needed for personal reasons, or even the destination we preferred to go to right then.

Seniority was most important during the holidays. I learned early on that my Christmases for the next fifteen years would be celebrated either onboard an airplane or in a foreign hotel. I didn't mind that so much, though, as most nice hotels would invite us—free of charge—to indulge in a sumptuous dinner.

But I also realized that December 24–25 are only dates, and later on when I married and had a daughter—when Pan Am had relaxed the rules on requiring stewardesses to be single—she didn't mind if we pretended Christmas was December 27–28 or 22–23.

CHAPTER 8

My Very First Day as a Stewardess

Before being able to go on your flight, we all had to first get inspected by the grooming supervisor. We were put on a scale—a couple of ounces more than our maximum allowed weight that was determined during our training would mean a warning note in our file. My maximum weight was 119. The next infraction on another preflight check would ground you until you lost it.

Then the grooming supervisor would pinch us to make sure we were wearing our regulation girdle, going almost down to the knees. This procedure lasted well into the seventies.

Then she checked our nails for regulation length and color—pink. Makeup, foundation, Revlon Persian Melon (a specific shade of pink) lipstick, and blue eyeshadow were a must. Regulation jewelry was one-single-pearl earrings, one small ring—remember, nobody was married—one small watch, and a bracelet. Shoes were plain black pumps with no less than a three-inch slim heel (dangerous to walk up and down the metal stairs to the airplane, as no ramp was available yet, and quite uncomfortable for walking miles just to reach the terminal and the gates). Our stockings had to have no snags; we always carried an extra pair in our tote bag, together with an extra pair of white gloves that had to be worn until after takeoff. Do you realize what passing fresh newspaper does to those little white gloves?

And for hair, we all had look-alike bobs with a Jackie Kennedy hat. The supervisor walked around us with a small pair of scissors in hand, in case a small hair was not sprayed into place.

On my first day of briefing, I held my breath almost the whole time. When I finally let go and turned around to walk out, she called me back. My heart stopped.

I was told I had a small spot on the back of my right shoe. They were newly polished, as we had to do before each flight. After questioning me, she declared it was probably due to my driving and shifting pedals. She advised me to tie some soft fabric around the back of my shoe to protect it from happening again, once I had bought new shoes.

My very first flight after I got my wings was to Robertsville, Liberia, West Africa. I had been called from standby for a twelve-day trip.

Twelve hours later at the destination, I was helping open the heavy front door and was hit by a wave of moist heat—and a supervisor standing at the top of the stairs. Her first words to me were that she would let my personal supervisor know that my hair was not groomed properly. Humidity was no excuse for frizzy hair.

Welcome to Pan American World of perfection.

My very first flight

Opening the door to face the supervisor!

CHAPTER 9

West Africa

Africa was worth all the problems getting there. In the sixties, Pan Am had two weekly flights on a DC8 to Robertsville, Liberia, on the west coast, where the crew had a four-day layover while the aircraft continued with a fresh crew for several stops all the way to the east coast. When that crew arrived back, they would have four more days until we made the return trip back with the aircraft.

The airport consisted of a small oblong reinforced hut, and the landing strip was a mowed area in a cleared section of the jungle in the middle of nowhere. Our accommodation was at a walking distance from the airport and was also a long building with open spaces between the roof and the walls for natural air conditioning. Unfortunately, the design was also convenient for all kinds of creatures to let themselves in.

During our short walk, we were surrounded by young local boys who were naked except for a small piece of cloth between their legs, holding up all kinds of wood carvings to our faces and calling out, "Missy, missy. Here, missy. Buy, missy. Very good, missy. You buy, very nice . . ."

I could not resist buying a pair of bookends in the shape of elephants with small ivory tusks. Bad idea. Within seconds, I was totally imprisoned by dozens of little boys calling for my attention. "Missy, me better. Missy, only two dollars, missy." The crew just laughed at me, and the captain "saved" me by giving them a few coins.

Later I also bought a small side table carved out as the shape of Africa, held up by the ivory tusks of two elephants. This caused me lots of problems, first to store it on the plane, then to carry it through the airport with my suitcase. No small carts had been invented yet, nor wheels on my heavy Samsonite.

But I managed to get the table back, and I still have it today.

Inside the hotel, the length of the building was divided by a hallway with rooms on both sides. Halfway down the hallway, a big opening on one side contained half a dozen shower stalls with lukewarm water coming down from a small hole in the ceiling. An inadequate piece of cloth hung halfway down in front of each stall. Next to them were a few sinks with something passing for a mirror. On the opposite side from the showers were half a dozen toilets with half pieces of wood on hinges for privacy. Hey, it could have been worse. In one small hotel in India that we saw, the facilities consisted of only a hole in the ground.

Except for the captain, the first officer, and the engineer, the crew was only females, so the men got ready before us. We tried our best to accomplish a regulation attire. These accommodations were a far cry from our regular ones in InterContinental Hotels, a chain owned by Pan Am in almost every large city of the world.

Our rooms also had space between the ceiling and the walls and the doors, resulting in nightly company of lizards. I had one on my pillow, looking at me when I woke up! I don't know who jumped the highest, he or me. I got used to them, though. They actually ate many of the other bugs of unknown species that liked to do nightly visits—and huge spiders.

This was our base for twelve days. Despite the lack of comfort, it was quite a popular trip because it gave us ten days off at home after such a long trip. Unless you were on call, as I was, you usually only got forty-eight hours off.

There were also a few advantages in being close to the Firestone Rubber Plantation, whose workers were only too happy to entertain six stewardesses and play tennis with the flight crew. They provided us with access to water skiing and exploring, drove us to nice beaches, and held wonderful barbecues. They had the best pineapples I've ever tasted. The crew used to bring dozens of steaks from America, and we raided the first-class liquor kits, which consisted of only big bottles at that time. They especially appreciated the Veuve Clicquot and La Grande Dame champagne. The hotel also provided us with wonderful dinners of freshly caught fish.

The Firestone Rubber Plantation was quite educational. We learned the whole process of how rubber was collected from rubber trees and the different preparation to make tires or other household items. It was well worth half a day of learning.

After our well-spent four days there, we walked next door to the airport, boarded the plane, and greeted our local passengers for a shuttle to Abidjan, Ivory Coast, Douala, Cameron, then Nairobi, Kenya. The next day we did a short turnaround to Dar es Salaam, Tanganyika, as it was still called at that time. The day after that, we did everything in reverse.

Most of our passengers wore colorful clothing and turbans holding all kinds of things, mostly pots and pans, food, pineapples; I must admit that keeping their heads straight gave them a regal posture. Many had live chickens or even goats with them. The women had their babies strapped to their backs, which created problems with the seat belts. The mothers bent forward in their seats and absolutely refused to remove their babies. It took some time to get everybody and the animals sort of secured.

In flight we ran into other problems, when some Africans would decide to sit down in the aisle to cook their meals on a small stove. Most refused to eat our prepared trays. One time a male passenger asked me where he could go to the bathroom, translated from "go pee." I pointed to the back of the airplane where the bathrooms were and said, "In the back." Big mistake. A few minutes later I saw, to my horror, that he had followed my words exactly, except he never opened the door. Needless to say, it was never a dull moment on these flights.

Back in Liberia another time, we had a small mechanical delay, so some of us wandered back to the nearby hotel while some stayed on the plane. One went to sit with her boyfriend.

The mechanical issue was resolved in less than a half hour, and we all returned. Or so we thought. When the stewardess with the boyfriend heard the engine starting, she realized we were ready to go. We all thought she was still on the airplane. She ran to the runway and waved frantically at the aircraft. The captain saw her and slowed down, and the engineer went down to the cargo hole, opened a trap, and pulled her up. No big deal in Africa.

CHAPTER 10

Nairobi, Kenya

After the trip to the Ivory Coast, where only a few passengers got off and a few boarded, we had another service on to Cameroon and arrived in Nairobi rather tired after all these stops, but had the whole next day off to spend there. In the morning, the InterContinental Hotel served us a big breakfast loaded with tropical fruits.

On one trip, our entertainment in this city consisted of a small safari in the Nairobi National Park, only a short drive away, with the cityscape of Nairobi as a backdrop. In this grassy landscape, we could spot lions, giraffe, rhino, and buffalo. For dinner, we all went to the Indian part of the city, where restaurants served some of the best curried dishes with close to fifteen condiments.

The next day we made the return flight to Robertsville, where we had another four days off. This time I was loaded with a whole elephant tusk that I had bought in the Nairobi market.

We had lounges on the planes at that time and even storage room. Thank God there was no TSA and no restrictions of endangered animals that we knew of at that time. The customs agents in New York just shook their heads when they saw us coming, dragging all kinds of unusual souvenirs. One time I brought home a whole zebra skin, and my biggest problem was fitting it in my car. At least I had a small station wagon. You wouldn't believe what we all came back with! Considering what another stewardess brought back from Teheran—a 12X10 handwoven Persian carpet; or do they call them "Iranian" carpets now?—at least my zebra wasn't as heavy as her carpet.

Through a friend who had friends in Monrovia, the capital of Liberia, I got an invitation from the president of Liberia, William Tubman, and Mrs. Tubman to attend the wedding of their daughter, Wilhelmina, on August 5, 1967. So many guests attended that only the closest family and friends and high-placed dignitaries got to go inside the palace. The rest of us—probably close to one thousand—wandered all over the gardens. We listened to several speeches through speakers. All in all, the event was quite different from what I expected and not so festive for me and the other guests who had to remain outside the palace.

The purchase

CHAPTER 11

First Vacation—Safari

Pan Am was the only carrier during the 1960s that had a flight around the world. The New York base flew the first half of it, and the California base the other half. My half had layovers in London, Beirut (what a beautiful city that was; our hotel overlooked the blue Mediterranean), then Bombay, Calcutta/ Karachi, Bangkok, and last Hong Kong.

My first vacation where I got to take advantage of my travel benefits was to take my mother on a safari. Living in cold Sweden, Africa was quite appealing and special. This one would be the first of many trips there. We ultimately went on two more different safaris for three weeks each.

First, a little history. In April 1964, Tanganyika united with Zanzibar to form the United Republic of Tanganyika and Zanzibar. The country was renamed the United Republic of Tanzania on October 29, 1964. The name was a blend of the names Tanganyika and Zanzibar.

Lake Manyara National Park, Serengeti National Park, and Ngorongoro Crater—all in Tanzania—are quite close together. Serengeti Park is on the border of Kenya and Maasai Mara National Reserve. The lions of Lake Manyara are a rarity among their own kind, being the only lions in the world to regularly climb trees and use the branches as a resting place. On one occasion, our jeep—with open roof—drove right under one of those trees with the lion sprawled on the branch, looking down on us just a few feet away from our heads. I didn't dare breathe when our white hunter told us to be still.

Fortunately, it was not the first time the lion had seen a car with people inside, and it was not his dinnertime, so after looking us over, he decided to go back to his nap. I did get a great picture, though, even with shaky hands. With no zoom (available only on professional cameras), the lion appears to be farther away, but I can assure you he was very close.

How many times did I wish I had a camera as there is now. I had to constantly change the black/white "roll"; note I didn't say "cartridge." My camera weighed several pounds and was quite cumbersome. The roll had to be threaded carefully and attached in a small slot, preferably in a dark place and not while shaking in a car. If the roll was to detach, bye-bye pictures. I had to replace my film in a hurry at times, hoping all the animals would wait for me to be ready.

We went on to Serengeti National Park, which is known for its massive annual migration of wildebeest and zebra when they moved north from their breeding grounds in the southern plains. The savannah landscape is mostly open grassland where you can see for miles but also home to the occasional grove of trees and others that stand solitary and shy, away from the crowds. Tall sausage trees have meter-long poisonous fruits that can weigh more than ten pounds each. You definitely don't want to stand under these trees and get hit by the weighty fruit. The baobab tree is also huge, with an unusual shape that reaches sixty feet tall and forty feet wide. The strangle vine begins as a vine before it eventually turns thick and woody. And finally, the umbrella tree, which has come to symbolize Africa, has a characteristic Y-shaped trunk that forms a delightful canopy.

Sometimes we were very close to herds of elephants, which was quite intimidating, but our hunter knew when to detect if we were not accepted by them and moved us away. But none of these beautiful animals had yet learned to be afraid of humans. Serengeti is also known for its cheetahs. We had the luck to see one run at high speed after an antelope. What a beautiful sight. The giraffes were also imposing when they curiously bent their long necks to inspect us closer. Our hunter didn't like the look of one rhino, so we wisely didn't stop there.

On another African vacation, mother and I camped in Amboseli National Park in neighboring Kenya—not in a tent, though; I wasn't that brave—but in a sort of hut. And glad was I to have solid walls when in the middle of the night a lion scratched at our door.

The next day we were honored with a dance of the Maasai warriors, all well over seven feet tall, in their red tunics and big jeweled collars.

Next we toured Ngorongoro crater, the world's largest inactive crater, one hundred square miles in size. Ngorongoro, being deep, forms a natural enclosure for elephants, rhinos, lions, leopards, buffaloes, and more.

It makes me cry that all this beauty might soon be a thing of the past, thanks to all the poachers. I feel guilty to have participated in that by buying their artifacts when I didn't know better. How could

I have ever guessed that overhunting would get so out of hand as to result in almost total eradication of several species?

Lion in the tree

CHAPTER 12

Treetops Lodge, Kenya

One memorable vacation in Africa was a stay at the Treetops Lodge in Kenya's Aberdare National Park. We were greeted by a guide called a white hunter—because he was a white man who was a professional big-game hunter—with a rifle who took us up a ladder to the wraparound deck of a big square building on stilts. Then the ladder was pulled up after us, and we were told we could not go down until the next day. The lodge was near a pretty big watering hole where many different species came to drink. The deck was furnished with big, comfortable lounge chairs, small side tables, and blankets for those who wanted to spend the night there. We also had a small room with bed and bathroom.

The staff was English and so was the service. In the middle of nowhere we were served a full English high tea by white gloved waiters as in the best hotel in London.

While we waited for the night and animals to seriously troupe in to the watering hole, our hunter entertained us on the rooftop with trained baboons. They are not as friendly as chimpanzees and have longer teeth than a lion. We were told to stay at some distance and keep our belongings secured, as they are fast thieves and pickpockets.

The buffet dinner the lodge prepared could easily be compared with a five-star restaurant. It was hard to remember we were in the middle of the jungle surrounded by wild animals.

After dinner we settled on the deck to wait for all of the animals to come drink at the watering hole. It would get quite cold in Africa after sundown, and waiters would supply us with hot tea or cocoa during the night.

Slowly, the different species arrived in flocks or as families, including elephants, water buffaloes, wildebeests, antelopes, hyenas, and then lions, leopards, and many more. Each group respected the others' need to drink at the watering hole. I found it amazing how animals understand the need for truce among themselves. Each one made not a sound, not a rush. If the hole became a little crowded, the arriving groups would wait patiently a little distance away.

I found out that they now have enlarged and modernized the lodge where we used to stay. Guests now have big, new bedrooms with a modern bath. Most of the wraparound deck is now enclosed by large windows, and a staircase has replaced the ladder. Yes, it did get cold, and yes, you can still see out to the watering hole from the windows, but it's not the same feeling of being in the jungle. The charm of the wild is gone.

CHAPTER 13

Luggage

Talking about vacation trips, do you know what can happen to your luggage once you check it for a flight? Be afraid. Be very afraid.

In the sixties, flying to Africa was not yet as organized as it is now. Each flight made several stops along the way. Most "airports" at the stops were still primitively built with what looked more like a hut than an airport building as we know it. You would not find any automatic equipment there nor any uniformed employees. A small booklet with carbon paper was handwritten on the spot with your name, flight number, and destination. One of these copies was given to you to retain, and another was glued on your luggage, which was brought out manually to the airplane. The last page was kept by the airline.

The cargo door remained open until all passengers had checked in. During that time other "things" could sneak in too, and did. Since the flight had several of these stops, you could end up with quite a variety of stowaways, which always caused delays upon arrival at your destination.

Snakes were often one of those things that found themselves onboard, as well as smaller curious animals and even smaller flying creatures. We always had to spray the aircraft before being allowed to open the doors, in case the smaller flying creatures were lethal insects.

Coming home one time, though, the delay was longer than usual, and passengers were told it would be awhile before they could get their luggage. We waited a long time, wondering what could be the problem.

We soon found out when we were called in to a side room to identify our luggage and belongings. The aircraft had been carrying back a few cages with monkeys, who were smart enough to find a way to open their cages and wander around the cargo hole. They were also smart enough to proceed to open all unlocked baggage, and that's when the party began! They had a ball, I'm sure, getting dressed in our clothes. Bras and panties were strewn everywhere.

It took every passenger quite a long time to find their own belongings; some went unclaimed. I wonder why. At that time it was quite embarrassing, but later—much later—I found the memory hilarious.

The recommendation our mothers used to give us, to always wear clean underwear in case of . . . really made the point here!

CHAPTER 14

The Best Way to Learn to Water Ski

I got assigned the twelve-day trips to Africa quite often. They almost came to feel like small vacations. I made several friends with families based in the area who enjoyed the easy life there. We played tennis, went to beautiful beaches, and took boat rides on the small waterways in the jungle.

On one of those layovers, some friends decided it was time for me to learn how to water ski. I got a quick lesson on how to hold tight and stay upright (yeah, right). Then I was put in the water while the boat slowly left with me attached to it.

On my first attempt, I never got up from my crouched position in the water. On my second attempt, I was dragged in a sitting position, which was not a good idea. By the third time I was finally able to stand fully up and was on my way.

After awhile I started to feel almost comfortable, that this was fun—at least until I looked down and saw I had company. I saw two sharks, one on each side of me like guardians. They were not huge sharks, maybe around four feet, but hey, they were sharks. My first response was to panic, but I quickly realized that was not a good idea. I decided the better plan was to concentrate on holding on for dear life and to panic later. I didn't dare let go of one hand to wave to my friends, who were in deep conversation. I screamed at the top of my lungs, but the sound of the motors covered it. The boat riders did look back a few times but interpreted all the faces I made as me having fun.

It seemed like forever before we finally headed home, still accompanied by my two sharks. We had almost stopped when my finned friends decided to go find lunch somewhere else. My friends praised me for not falling and only laughed at me when I told them I'd had no other choice.

CHAPTER 15

How I Learned Italian

I wasn't feeling at all well when I left home to fly to Rome, Italy, but I wasn't about to lose nineteen hours' of flight pay simply because I didn't feel 100 percent! After all, it was a night flight and, hopefully, almost all of the passengers would fall asleep after their dinner.

Mercifully, the flight was uneventful, and I made it to the hotel without incident. I jumped into the shower in my hurry to get to bed, and that's when I noticed in the bathroom mirror—much to my horror—I had bunches of red spots all over my body! Shocked, I realized I also had the beginnings of a fever. What on earth was wrong with me?

Panicking, I called the front desk and asked them to send up a doctor. When he arrived at the door to my room, he stayed there, as if not daring to enter. Immediately, I knew what he was thinking. I informed him I'd had chicken pox as a child and had gotten vaccinated for smallpox, so it was unlikely to be either of those. He told me calmly, from the safety of my door, he was sending me away for fourteen days' quarantine in a hospital in a convent run by nuns.

Shortly, masked ambulance drivers took me away via the hotel's back entrance, to avoid anyone coming into contact with me (and so I didn't scare the other guests!), and I was told Pan Am would be notified.

I was eventually diagnosed with chicken pox. I didn't realize until then you could catch the disease more than once, and it was a pretty bad case at that. For the first ten days of my fourteen, I had a raging fever and itched like crazy! The same two nuns looked after me day and night throughout my quarantine; I knew them only as "Sister." They brought me cool, soothing ointment for my rash and blisters, and made sure I didn't scratch at my face by covering my hands with soft woollen mittens.

The two sisters spoiled me rotten with everything they could think of. They brought all kinds of broths and soups and fresh, handmade pasta (of course!), and they talked to me nonstop as they insisted I eat more to keep my strength up. That was most definitely not a problem—once I tasted their delicious food, I was hooked! They made all their meals at the convent from vegetables they grew themselves in the lush gardens and eggs collected fresh from the chickens every morning. When I began feeling a little better, I would go out picking fresh apricots and figs in the small garden onsite. Now, I had never really liked milk, but when the sisters gave me a taste, fresh from the convent's cow, I literally begged for more! Seeing my growing appetite made them laugh, and I could tell they were happy to see me eat so healthily after only a few days. At first they had only served me small portions, but once I began cleaning my plate, they started to give me more and more.

For someone who was so sick, I managed to gain twelve pounds and actually struggled to get back into my uniform after my month at the convent hospital. I stayed home another two weeks after the sisters finally released me, and even then I barely made it down to my maximum weight—thank heavens I'd been well below it to start with! With the two sisters talking at me all the time, I quickly learned to communicate with them pretty well by the end of the first week. With the help of my fluent French and the constant babble of one or the other of my constant companions, I soon picked up the everyday conversational language.

The ever-friendly sisters would ask endless questions about my life "flying all over the world" and the differences between all the exotic countries I visited and the people in each place. I came to realize the "Hospital for Contagious Diseases" was entirely within their convent, and they never got to venture beyond its walls. That was why they were so curious about the world outside.

Once I was no longer contagious, I asked if I might call my mother. That was not as easy as it should have been, as the only telephone was in the priest's office and was not available to mere sisters. I asked them if I could talk to the father, and he then made the effort to come talk to me. We had a lovely chat, but he explained that no woman had ever set foot in his sacred place, and it would be quite impossible for me to do so. However, I did manage to persuade him to allow me to let my poor mother know what had become of me and that I was all right; I knew she would be so worried.

The father informed me he would order an international call to the US for the very next day; back in 1960, it wasn't quite as easy as simply dialing another country—it could take two or three hours of waiting just to get a free line.

I was so relieved when I finally got to speak with my dear mother, especially since Pan Am had not bothered to inform her as to my whereabouts or why I had not been in touch for so long! And, I later learned, the doctor had said nothing to anyone—he had been silenced (bribed?) by the hotel, as they feared quarantine, which would have devastated their business.

My guess was that communications were not that easy and, after a couple of weeks, Pan Am simply assumed I'd gone home. Unfortunately, they called my poor mother to ask why I had missed several of my trips! As you can imagine, that scared the heck out of the poor woman, who thought Pan Am had managed to lose me.

She was beyond relieved to hear from me and glad I was getting better and would be home in a couple more weeks once my blisters were gone.

I was so grateful for the priest going against tradition to allow me to call home, and he was delighted too, when I told him my mother had no idea why I had never returned home and had been worried half to death by Pan Am calling to ask where I was.

The father visited me in my hospital bed several times during my stay, and attempted on more than one occasion to convert me to Catholicism. We had some good, long, lively discussions, but after awhile, he came to realize that even though I wasn't much for religion, I still had a good conscience and followed the right paths. He did tell me, bless him, that in a way, he thought I "believed" more than many people.

By the time I left the convent, all the talking with the priest and the two sisters had made me fluent in Italian. I think picking up languages is just in my genes; my father spoke nine, including the notoriously difficult Greek and Romanian.

Once I was back at work for Pan Am, I took lessons in airline and technical language, as well as qualifying in Italian, and I continued to communicate with my sisters at the convent by letter for several years afterward.

So, my chicken pox episode didn't turn out so bad after all. I gained two incredibly sweet new friends and a brand-new language. I sure did miss all the delicious food, though, and I never managed to find milk with that unique nutty taste ever again.

CHAPTER 16

Becoming a Purser

I was a quick learner, very fast and organized, and could see immediately what needed to be done. I picked up all the tricks and learned how to make the impossible work. After about eight months, I knew enough to pass the test to become a purser, in charge of the service. I would still have the responsibilities I did before, with the addition of overseeing the whole service in both classes, writing reports on special problems, handling carry-ons and special requests, as well as filling out lots of paperwork. The good thing about having this job was that I could make a service the way I liked it. The aircraft was mine—at least the cabin, not the cockpit. Although many times the captain would call me to check if this or that was OK with me, or to ask how I felt about doing something differently.

The bad thing was that the buck stopped with me. In a crisis or whenever any problem arose, all eyes were on me and waited for me to come up with a solution. Somehow I managed to keep my flights in full control and was told I had eyes in the back of my head. Very few, if any, discrepancies went unnoticed. The good workers liked to fly with me, and the bad or lazy ones did not. I always caught them.

As a purser, I had the "honor" to carry heavy manuals, announcement books, paperwork, and also all the heavy serving utensils we used onboard, such as tongs, serving forks and spoons, a corkscrew, spatulas, a cheese knife, the one-and-a-half foot carving set, and all silver-plated lead. Believe me, it felt like lead when I carried each piece up and down the stairs in a tight skirt and high heels. These serving pieces had to be transported back and forth, as they were too expensive to leave on the aircraft unattended.

I was also responsible for all the monies collected from the sales of drinks and duty free. This was the worst part of my job because we collected currencies from all over the world, and it was a nightmare to have to convert them to US dollars and get the final count to match with what we sold after the inventory.

Originally, as I mentioned, I had to be talked into becoming a stewardess by a good friend. The irony is that, by the time I finally started flying, she had quit. She assured me she tried to stay but was overcome with a growing fear of flying that got worse with every takeoff and landing.

CHAPTER 17

Favorite Places

Often I'm asked to name my favorite city. But I find it impossible to give a straight answer. Do I want to eat? Do I want to shop? Do I want to relax? Do I want sightseeing?

Even those four answers are divided by "what." What do I want to eat, what do I want to shop, what do I want to see?

France, Austria, and even Germany are high on the list for pastries and desserts. For chocolates, I'd recommend France, Belgium, and Germany. The best tempura is, of course, from Japan, and wiener schnitzel from Germany. And you can't find a better fish soup anywhere than in Nice, France. I've been so spoiled that I can't eat pasta in any country other than Italy. With that said, I have found exceptional restaurants in every city.

Of course, Paris comes first for shopping for clothing, but Rome is a worthy second.

For gifts, every city has their specialties. I'd recommend precious stone jewelry from South America; pearls from Japan (very expensive), Korea (very cheap), or China; and all kinds of things from India. At the gold market in Beirut, the walls of the stores were covered floor to ceiling with 18K gold jewelry. No matter what it was, sellers grabbed a handful of it, put it on the scale, and gave us a ridiculously low price. (Gone are those days!) South America had the same system but with genuine stones and beads of all sizes hanging on strings, everything from jade to amethyst, coral, rubies, emeralds, and turquoise. I could go on and on. If you had a picture of some jewelry, they could replicate it and you could pick it up on your next flight. Seoul and Beijing did the same but with pearls. Our Christmas gifts from all those different countries were much appreciated by our friends.

As for the cities themselves, they all have their wonders and beauty in different ways. I especially fell in love with Beirut, Lebanon, on my first flight around the world with Pan American, especially the people and the blue of the Mediterranean directly outside the window of our rooms in the Phoenicia Hotel.

In Rome, I loved to walk around and admire all the beautiful fountains, churches, and buildings, even though the cobblestone sidewalks were torture in heels. But no decent woman and especially Pan American stewardesses would dare wear flats.

On a three-day layover in Italy, some of us took a train to Sicily, the ruins of Pompeii, and the volcano Etna that towers over the city of Sicily. I had newfound respect for volcanoes when I saw the destruction Mount Vesuvius leashed on the ancient town and citizens of Pompeii. The active volcano Etna has erupted a half dozen times in the twentieth century alone, threatening nearby towns.

Bangkok, Thailand, was lovely with all its temples, and I loved the mountainous terrain of Rio de Janeiro as well as the gardens in Japan. Every city has one of my favorite things.

Bangkok earned a reputation with us for taking our orders for silk clothing, sewing them during the night, and having the garments ready before we left. The skilled seamstresses anticipated our arrival in the hotel and eagerly and efficiently took our measurements. The garments usually fit, and if one didn't, we could bring it back on our next trip. Those were the perks of being a stewardess.

Dubai, in the United Arab Republic, was a lengthy fifteen-hour flight with several services. But the most unbelievable architecture in the world was there, and nothing seemed impossible. To this day, their tall, curved, weird-shaped buildings are unique in the world.

Dubai even features man-made islands in the sea—the Palm Islands, which will eventually be a set of three artificial islands with beautiful housing, one of which is already complete. This island, Palm Jumeirah, has long, thin individual islands shaped like the fronds of a palm tree and encircled by another artificial island. The ambitious project was built with sand dredged from the Persian and Arabian Ocean floors, compacted, and surrounded by millions of tons of rocks for protection. I flew to Dubai when construction first began on those projects and saw every building taking form from the desert sand. Many of them taller than the Empire State Building, some buildings have apartments that can be rotated to always face the sun. Some have elevators to transport residents' cars up to their private garage in the sky, next to their apartment.

I haven't seen anything like that in other cities; it's almost futuristic. Burj Al Arab Jumeirah, the most expensive and luxurious hotel in the world with a golf course on the roof where Tiger Woods has played, is in Dubai. We tried to visit, but they would not let us in without reservations.

The Dubai Mall contains 1,200 luxury stores and the biggest aquarium in the world. Our hotel was adjacent to it.

Another part of town had an indoor area where you could ice skate and ski down snow-covered hills. Still another area featured an indoor beach with waves for surfing. In a separate outdoor area, fountains danced in hundreds of different colors and patterns. Anything you can imagine, they could build it. The streets are kept clean, with flowers everywhere.

The desert safari is an unforgettable tourist attraction. It's not far outside Dubai, where the desert is as far as you can see, with camels roaming around. You can ride the camels and also tour in a closed jeep with a driver who takes great pleasure in scaring you to death. With no seat belts and no handle to grab, he drives at the fastest impossible speed, up and down the moving sand dunes as the sand almost covers the car like waves. You are positively sure the car will turn upside down any minute. The more you scream, the more the driver laughs. You can barely stand on shaky legs after that.

Then they take you to a small oasis where you can ride camels or visit some Bedouin tents while waiting for a wonderful barbecue, with music and belly dancers around a fire. What a wonderful day.

Tourists have to respect certain rules in clothing and behaviors, which change over time, but not as serious as what we females experienced in the city of Abu Dhabi in the United Arab Emirates. There we were not allowed to eat in the restaurant (sinful women) with the pilots and had to hide behind a big screen. We were given a chador (a garment that covers the head and face) if we wanted to go out.

While we waited for our pickup the next morning, in full uniform, a big screen was again placed near us to hide us from the residents.

Damascus 1966

CHAPTER 18

Around (Half) the World

I especially liked that I worked for Pan Am when it was the only airline with an around-the-world flight. Our first stop was London. Then Beirut with two days off in the beautiful InterContinental Hotel.

Each stewardess always carried a cocktail dress for our dinners in the fancy restaurants. We always had to keep up Pan Am's image of glamour, always dressed in either our uniform when on duty or in a dress and heels for sightseeing. These were the days when people dressed up.

The worst was to carry all that in a heavy Samsonite suitcase— luggage was not lightweight in those days and didn't even have the luxury of wheels. Those and foldable carts came years later.

From Beirut we went to Bombay, India, where the hotel The Taj Mahal Palace looked like it had come directly out of the "1,001 Arabian Nights" fairy tale. Its gold dome beckoned us in to enjoy the fine woodwork, unique and elegant room layouts, and gothic arched doorways.

When the political party Shiv Sena came into power in 1995, Bombay was renamed Mumbai. The traffic and noise in this town is unreal. Three-wheeled vehicles draped in fabric all around, motorcycles, and cars—honking all the way—blended with dogs and sacred cows in the streets. The cows had priority, walking everywhere, stopping traffic in the middle of the road. I swear they knew exactly what they were doing.

The women are beautiful in their colorful and gold embroidered saris, wearing gold earrings, necklaces, and bracelets. We had a great time shopping and sightseeing in Bombay, and also had the best spicy tandoori chicken that brought tears to our eyes.

Our next stop was Bangkok, Thailand. The streets have a strong special smell, a mix of all the different spices sold on the sidewalks and foods being prepared and served all around you. This ancient trading town features the stunning Wat Arun temple—Temple of Dawn—with a golden spire that reaches over 225 feet tall and is beautifully lit up at night. The temple sits alongside the Chao Phraya River, which weaves through the city—reminding me of the Seine River winding through Paris—and features a floating market. The Grand Palace, built in 1782, is another highlight, with its intricate oriental architecture and emerald Buddha carved from a single block of emerald.

You'd need weeks to explore it all. I did climb up the steps of the Temple of Dawn, which were difficult enough, high and narrow, but the way down was even more scary. I had to do it backward. Of course, it didn't help that I was wearing my required high heels. I also saw the 150-foot long reclining Buddha, covered in gold, in Bangkok's temple complex.

Then on to Hong Kong, the scariest landing I ever saw (from the cockpit). The pilot handled the plane expertly, so that was no problem, but seeing the obstacles he faced was a little too much information for me. The landing strip at Hong Kong's Kai Tak International Airport, which has been closed since 1998, was located in a bowl between two mountains. The pilot had to fly over the mountain, but immediately over it, he had to fly down the other side to where the ocean is. The ground and concrete buildings below us were so close, I thought we would scrape their rooftops. Within a very short distance were two landing strips, half in the ocean. And after one of the shortest runways was another mountain. If the plane flew too low, it would take a dip in the ocean. And if it came in too fast, it would crash into the mountain.

The takeoff was even worse: if the plane didn't leave the runway fast enough, again the ocean was waiting, and if it didn't lift soon enough, the mountain would take the blow.

By the time we were safely on the ground, we were more than exhausted and jet lagged, and all that counted was a good bed and a full ten hours of sleep.

Ahead of us, we had the way back home, with more adventures waiting.

Baalbek, Lebanon 1965

Jupiter Temple in Baalbek, Lebanon

Pigeon Grotto, Beirut 1965

CHAPTER 19

Shorter Layovers

The best layovers happened between the end of 1960 and 1970, when flights were not daily and aircrafts were smaller, such as DC8s and Boeing 707s. When the airbus, 777, 767, and 747 came in service with hundreds of passengers and twice-daily flights, our layovers were shortened to regulation twelve hours at the destination unless it was a night flight to Europe, in which case we got the extra night.

The driving time to and from the airports could take several hours and shorten our hours of rest. Paris, London, and Tokyo airports were all outside the city, or else our hotel was outside, and we usually arrived right on time for the morning commute. In some places, we ended up with barely eight hours in the hotel. By the time we took a shower, rested, ate, and got our hair and makeup ready for the next flight, our sleeping time could be down to only six hours. Forget leaving the hotel then.

On most European flights, we arrived in the midmorning after we had practically "walked across the pond." We had been up over twenty-four hours by then and had the choice of sleeping or going shopping for items we couldn't do without.

Then we would eat and sleep until wake-up time. Unless we were in Tokyo or Dubai, by this time we had been up for more than forty-eight hours. But then we usually did get an extra day.

CHAPTER 20

Moscow

Moscow was like another world. The hotel felt like a prison, with guards on each floor. They were at your door the minute you opened it, asking where you were going. They kept our passports and house keys with them.

I spent my fiftieth birthday there, feeling sorry for myself. But the food was good, including vodka and caviar, and the airline arranged a tour of the city for us. I was impressed by the iconic Kremlin building, with its onion-shaped turrets and bold colors. Nearby was the famous Red Square, which featured a ceremonial changing of the guard and Eternal Flame. The square also housed Lenin's tomb, where his preserved body is on display—still a tourist attraction even though he died in 1924.

I noticed a great contrast between the dark and gloomy streets and the subway that looked like a palace with huge crystal chandeliers and gold and paintings at every station.

It was extremely cold both times I was there.

CHAPTER 21

Stowaway

The flights to Tokyo, Japan, were a grueling twenty hours, plus a date change and twelve-hour time difference backward, then a day forward coming home. On the flights we served two full dinners, lunch, and breakfast. Snacks were always available to passengers.

I did like Tokyo and the time off we got at home after the flight. I flew these routes quite a bit in 1974 when Hello Kitty became a craze with my daughter and her friends. Yes, four years after my employment the rules changed and we were allowed to get married, and a few more years after, my daughter was "legally" produced, one month after the ban on pregnancies was lifted.

Unfortunately, Pan Am grounded me for ten months without pay before we got the insurances arranged. Because of that, a funny— actually not so funny—event happened at the hospital. Pan American medical insurance refused to pay for my delivery on the grounds that my daughter's name was "not listed as family" on my insurance. How could she possibly be listed before she was born? It took a good while to fight that, but they finally realized it was a stupid argument.

Back to Hello Kitty, before she made her appearance in America and became famous, I was bringing back a few souvenirs that all of my daughter's friends wanted to have too. Many of her friends begged me to bring more back. For a while I even got worried that customs would think I had a business reselling these trinkets. I brought the first video game, with Pac-Man and Mario, but at that time kids didn't understand what it was all about. Little did we all know how that industry would grow and grow.

One time, when my daughter was six years old, she was sad to see me fly off to Tokyo for five days, two in flight and two and a half on layover. She had also heard me talking about the city, especially the unique food and the shopping. She begged to come with me. She had already learned to behave well on an airplane, and our passenger count was light. I thought, why not, and decided to bring her along.

We had an uneventful flight. She sat quietly playing in her seat and reading and eating properly and sleeping. She knew she would never come back on an airplane if she was not good.

We got there and had a marvelous time. She totally ignored her jet lag and the twelve-hour difference making the night the day and the day the night.

She enjoyed the different way of life, the kimono-clad ladies, and the food. She quickly learned to use the chopsticks, to the delight of all the servers, and fell in love with the tempura.

We ventured to the underground subway, beautifully clean and with employees in white gloves whose job was called "pushers." Their only job was to push you inside the train so they could close the doors.

My daughter was amazed with the huge display of everything Hello Kitty and was sad not to be able to carry more home.

On the day of the return flight, when we arrived at the airport, I was told that the Japanese airline had gone on strike and we were unexpectedly overbooked with all their passengers. I almost fainted; this could not happen. I couldn't possibly leave her there.

Thank God security was not invented yet. She followed me and the crew all the way to our 747 aircraft without any problem. Following the pilots' union rule for long-distance flight time, this airplane was equipped with bunks for them in the cockpit to take turns resting. They also had an extra pilot.

I took her straight up to the upper lounge and to the cockpit, while the pilots were still at their briefing in the terminal. I put her in the corner of the bottom bunk with her suitcase, hiding her, and told her not to move until I got back to her.

As the purser on that flight, I got busy with ordering extra provisions and rearranging the services. I forgot about her until I heard an announcement from the loudspeaker. It was the captain talking: "We have a situation up here. Could the purser please come up?"

Oh no. Would this be my last flight? I rushed up our winding staircase, thanking heaven that the captain was one of the good old guys.

I apologized profusely that I hadn't explained the situation earlier and assured him I would put her in one of our crew seats after takeoff. I also promised to serve him his dinner before the passengers if he so desired.

He answered me that it might be a problem since the "young lady" refused to leave the bunk. Like I said, Pan Am had some understanding guys. He kindly strapped her in their extra pilot seat, and she got to see the takeoff from Tokyo.

After takeoff, the stewardess assigned to the small upstairs galley put her to work folding some napkins and made her a small bed to sleep, behind the last row of seats of the lounge. My daughter still remembers this trip as one of the best.

Bangkok, Thailand—Grand Palace—Alexandra

CHAPTER 22

How It Works

In the beginning of commercial flights, many passengers were convinced—now they know better—that all stewardesses did was smile and say, "Fasten your seat belts." And all the rest magically appeared.

The bigger the airplane, the more passengers we needed to serve. The more passengers, the more work the flight became. And that didn't take into consideration the effect of jet lag and missing sleep every other night. The number-one problem was how/where to store everything needed to replicate a five-star restaurant's kitchen. And what to do with all the trash. We couldn't simply open the door and throw out a big bag. If we didn't stack all plastic and paper cups, crush each box and can, and put everything else away in exactly the same place we got it from, we would drown, especially if we had more than one main service.

Another fact that may surprise younger people today is that many people in the 1960s and 1970s smoked on the planes. So every service we did was performed through a cloud of secondhand smoke.

Thanks to my French language–speaking skills, I had the pleasure to be the purser on the inaugural flight of the 747 airplane between New York's JFK Airport and Paris's Orly Airport in January 1970.

It was filled with reporters from several countries. The first airplane with two decks was able to carry over four hundred passengers, depending on the configuration of seats. I opened over one hundred bottles of champagne that night.

We started with twenty stewardesses for the two classes and upstairs services, but barely a year later the count went down to eighteen, then sixteen. Another year later, only fourteen stewardesses served the same number of passengers, and the number finally ended up with only eleven. We had to be extremely organized and fast. As soon as one service was finished, we had to immediately start reloading the beverage carts and ovens. All the while passengers never stopped for a minute asking for yet another drink or bag of peanuts. Before landing, we had to take inventory of all items used and left and hope the numbers would match our money. This part I hated.

If you are not convinced yet that there was more to our jobs than "fasten your seat belt," we were also there for passengers who fainted, had a heart attack, needed CPR, or were ready to deliver a baby.

On that note, let me explain why the meal service on a L-1011 aircraft is a nightmare. The aircraft's galley is on a floor beneath you, and all your carts are put in an elevator for the service. All the meals are cooked downstairs, and everything else you need after takeoff is there as well. All I can say is, you had better not forget something.

In order not to crowd the aisles, each item had a particular spot. And each item had to be returned to that same spot. If the elevators malfunctioned, which did happen only too often, that was another story.

One time we did a whole first-class service through the emergency trapdoor between the galley and the first-class aisle. The service was not as lavish as with carts, but most passengers were grateful to get anything. But there are always some who will complain, and those were upset that our service wasn't fast enough or they didn't get seconds of this or that. It's quite difficult to balance a tray of appetizers with one hand while holding on to a ladder.

First of all, let me tell you that when you board from the front door and look down the cabin to the back, you cannot see the end of it. Two aisles run the whole distance, starting with two front rows of first-class seats divided in a 2–2–2 pattern, for a total of twelve passengers. Then comes what Pan Am called business class, with six rows in a 2–4–2 pattern, for a total of forty-eight passengers, and 42 rows of economy class in a 2–5–2 pattern, for an additional 378 passengers.

Two aisles are a plus, but the five passengers in one row are squashed together, particularly the one in the middle of the middle section, who has to climb over two persons to get out, whether he goes left or right. He is in a bad mood from the beginning, and I can't say I blame him.

For us, there is a bright side. When the service is over, we can take turns disappearing to the lower galley with the elevator and scream or cry, however we feel in the moment.

Unfortunately, the elevators did break down more often than we wished, but the show had to go on. I recall on one flight when the elevator was nonfunctional that we managed to pass all the first-class meals on trays through the emergency escape route from the lower galley. It opened on the first-class floor between the right aisle.

But unfortunately, that didn't work for economy class, where the only way to bring up the dozens of carts to the cabin was with the elevators. That's when we had to improvise. We formed a human chain to carry the trays filled with just the meal casseroles. We could pile about twenty-four on one big tray. Then some of us made up big trays with Coke or water, then trays with coffee. The result was not great either for them or us, but at least they didn't have to starve.

CHAPTER 23

L-1011, The Real Service

Let's pretend now that everything works, including the elevators, and you have your eight knowledgeable stewardesses, two positioned at each of the four doors of economy class. You the passenger are seated comfortably, right?

Have you ever realized that your stewardess has to be a mathematician to manage a service in an L-1011 in the shortest (im) possible time? And most of you are probably not aware of the skills one must possess to maneuver four meal carts weighing over one hundred pounds, and four beverages carts, even heavier, all in a synchronized manner.

OK, ready, GO! The dance begins, with stewardess #1 on the left food cart followed by stewardess #2 on the beverage cart. On the right side, stewardess #3 on the right food cart is followed by stewardess #4 on the beverage cart. From the back, stewardess #5 on the food cart will start from the back left side followed by stewardess #6 on the beverage cart, both working their way up to the middle of the cabin. On the right side, stewardess #7 on the food cart will follow suit with stewardess #8 on the beverage cart, and hopefully all eight of them will arrive, at best, almost at the same time. Sounds easy and logical!

The trick to deliver the tray to the middle person in the middle section of five is not to fall on the lap of the first two passengers when you try to reach the third, the one in the middle of the middle, with your arms trying to deploy like an octopus and a smile on your face because the two passengers you are leaning on do not appreciate that. Between you and me, if that bothers them, would it really be too much to take the darn tray and pass it over? Are you still with me?

But wait! Then stewardess #2 will back up to the left door near the galley, followed by stewardess #1 with the empty meal cart, and bless the galley attendant who has brought up fresh carts. Stewardess #1 starts a little toward the aisle followed by stewardess #2 to give room for stewardess #4 and stewardess #3 to get to their fresh meal carts. Same thing will happen from the back two doors. And the dance continues until all passengers have been fed.

Then stewardess #1 and stewardess #3 start picking up the trays while stewardesses #2 and #4 go around with coffee and pray they won't be asked for a Coke or something they don't carry now.

Unless a passenger—usually from a middle seat—decides he has to visit the toilet right now! Attention, attention all stewardesses, stop the dance and move the two-hundred-pound carts on this side of the aisle all the way back to the starting point to let the passenger by . . . with the regulation smile on your face!

Sorry, folks, the dance to be continued.

Now that all the passengers have been served tea and coffee and you name it, you continue picking up the empty trays. But why oh why do the passengers love to pile everything to look like the tower of Pisa?

You cannot put the tray back in the small slot allotted to it with a shaky pyramid. So with one hand you have to destroy the edifice so it can fit back in the cart, all the while the next passenger who cannot wait one more minute starts piling up his tray on top of your cart! Can't he see I only have two hands and no room on my cart, and realize I would finish even faster if he didn't pile everything possible on it?

Of course this observation stays in my head, but I have promised myself that one day, I will say it loud and clear!

CHAPTER 24

Celebrities and Their Behavior

Since I'm in a complaining mode, let's talk pet peeves and some passenger behavior. Some can drive a stewardess crazy.

Let's say 11B pushes his call button, usually when you just sat down on your jump seat after the meal service to eat some cold leftover food. The call is also usually way up front if you are in the back. 11B asks what kind of drinks we have. Seriously? After we've just finished serving three beverage services? Did he think I took a parachute and went shopping? You want to answer, "Same as thirty minutes ago; we don't reprovision in flight," but you don't and store that phrase in your mind along with the other ones you intend to say aloud someday. To appease him, you go through the whole list again. He wants a Coke. You go back to the galley, get the Coke, and walk the long aisle back to 11B. Then 11A says, "Me too," leaving off the word please. What stopped him from asking that before? Did he think I couldn't remember two Cokes at once? I could cover several pages with all the stupid questions we get.

I finally get back to my now definitely cold leftovers. That's how we keep our figures.

Let's talk celebrities who were a big deception.

On one flight, a famous American actress was sitting in first class, and her son, maybe seven or eight at the time, was in economy class with a nanny. The problem was that he constantly ran up and down the aisles and also to first class where he stood around and over the passengers, bothering them. I brought him back and politely, with a smile plastered on my face, told Miss Actress that her son was to stay where he belonged.

After the fourth time, I may have been less polite, and she was outraged, storming after me to remind me who she was. Well, I wouldn't brag about it right now if I were her. This was just after her very first film. At least I got support from my passengers who said they couldn't work/sleep with him around. She traded seat with the nanny and let me know she was going to write to the company about me.

My second disappointment with a celebrity (two in forty-five years is not bad, after all) was with Jackie Kennedy, soon-to-be Onassis. She boarded with an economy ticket, which surprised me. I found out shortly after the reason why. She had a reputation for being stingy and not very nice with the workers.

She asked to speak with the purser—me—and demanded to be upgraded to first class. I would have done it if it hadn't been presented as an obligation. I played dumb, apologizing that the agent must have issued her a wrong ticket, and I would immediately have it changed to a first-class one, with my best glued-on regulation smile.

I went to the ticket agent and was told she did that all the time, wanting to be upgraded for free. She of all the passengers surely could afford a first-class ticket. That didn't sit well with me.

I went back and told her first class was full, that she would have to wait until all were onboard to see if there would be an empty seat. Luckily, there wasn't, and I wasn't about to dislodge a full-paying passenger to put her there for free. I apologized, although I shouldn't have had to, really. For the rest of the flight she refused to be served by me. You can't win them all. I have upgraded many deserving passengers in my time, but not because they felt entitled to it.

One time after takeoff, a high and mighty businessman sitting in economy was complaining about having to sit next to an old woman who was reading her Bible with her reading light on. He insisted on being moved to first class. I told him I would see what I could do. I checked on the situation in the front of the plane and came right back with my glued-on regulation smile. I then asked the lady to come with me. The poor thing wondered what would happen to her. I took her to an empty first-class seat and told her to enjoy it, read all she wanted, and enjoy the flight. She was so grateful and gave me the biggest smile, I felt good about my decision.

I came back to the man and, again with my best regulation glued-on smile, explained that I didn't want him to be bothered with her light during the long flight and had therefore moved her to another seat.

On a flight to Nice, South of France, we had a royal prince on board, along with several of his friends. He'd been studying in America and was still very young then. They had been assigned seats all over first class.

They were talking quite loudly to each other across the cabin and annoying the other passengers. I told him to be a little more quiet but got only faces behind my back. It got worse when dessert came and the prince decided it would be funny to throw projectiles of pieces of cake with his spoon over the heads of the other passengers. Then his immature friends responded in kind. When some innocent passenger was hit, I had to intervene. "I'm very sorry, your highness," I told him, "but this behavior doesn't become you, and you all have to quiet down and stop throwing food."

He thought I was a party pooper and made more grimaces behind my back. Then the group got up and went to economy class, where they started bothering them for a while. On my demand, the captain made an announcement that everybody should go back to their seats and fasten their seat belts. That and all the champagne they drank helped because eventually they all fell asleep. He did apologize to me on disembarking.

I also had the pleasure of serving great celebrities. Charlton Heston and his wife once rode on a plane with me, traveling with his friend John Wayne and his wife. My, they both were so tall they had to bend their heads to clear the door opening of the airplanes. They were the nicest and easiest passengers, both wonderful couples. Bob Hope was also a joy as a passenger. He entertained the whole cabin during a flight.

And then there was Maureen O'Hara, who was married to one of our captains who owned an island in the Caribbean. She often shuttled back and forth with us. She would talk about her filming days without an ounce of high mightiness. I appreciated her humility in flying commercial rather than going the way of many celebrities who now fly with their own jets and pilots.

We also were privileged to fly with Gloria Swanson, who was known in her younger years as the "Queen of the Screen." She was in the first class of our fairly new 747 a few years before she passed away in 1983. She was on a special diet and had to eat a fruit plate every couple of hours. She liked to tell us stories of her life as a big actress during the silent film era and how she had won an Academic Award Recognition and a Golden Globe for the 1950 film *Sunset Boulevard*. She was married six times and had many lovers. Among them was John F. Kennedy's father, Joseph P. Kennedy. She was a real star but so very nice and sweet. A famous line from her award-winning movie captured the essence of her life: "I am still big; it's the pictures that got small."

CHAPTER 25

A Stewardess Has to Be Resourceful

Another requirement of the stewardess job is resourcefulness. For example: a flight might not be full to begin with, but just before the doors close for departure, a group of eighteen passengers from a canceled flight are put on your flight. The issue is that we have already loaded on the correct amount of food for the original number of passengers. The captain doesn't want to delay the plane and have to write the company that the reason he delayed the flight was for eighteen missing economy meals, causing the whole plane to then be late for arrival at destination and having to get new departure paperwork.

Did I mention previously that as a purser the buck stops with me? So with confidence, the pilot tells me, "You'll find a way." An easy solution would seem to be to donate our crew meals, but the airline figures there's always enough leftovers for us and doesn't generally add our meals over and above the passenger count onboard. The pilots always have meals accounted for, because their union says they have to eat or they won't have the strength to land the plane! If I insist on ordering and waiting for an additional eighteen meals to get loaded, which will delay the plane, I'll be getting a call on my layover or when I get home to ask why I caused a fifteen-minute delay, which means costing the airline money. They will not want to hear that I was missing eighteen economy meals. That is not a good enough reason for them. Plus I'll get a black mark on my record and have to deal with an angry captain for the rest of the trip.

So our solution is to cut all the portions in half and feed half of the cabin first. When we collect this first batch of trays and bring them back to the galley, two stewardesses grab them and frantically collect all unopened items, clean the trays, and make new ones with the leftovers. The second half of the cabin may wonder what kind of weird service this is, but we continue to serve them with big smiles on our faces, and no one will be the wiser.

In first class the meals are a little easier since they're not pre-portioned but instead come in big foil pans that normally serve six. In a pinch, we can divide the portions into eight instead of six. Passengers who might remember the portion they got on a previous flight probably chalk up the difference to the airline trying to save a bit of money. Most probably don't even notice at all.

CHAPTER 26

Air Marshals

Most people today are aware of how much security airports now have to prevent acts of terrorism on airplanes. But I can tell you, we could have used some better security in the earlier era. Hijackings have decreased significantly in the modern era, but between 1968 and 1972 there were several hijacking situations, so Pan Am had us attend special training. We were trained in how to detect probable problem passengers, with our primary goal to protect the cockpit using our carts as blockades. By then the cockpits were locked and we needed a password to get in. What a pain whenever they wanted a cup of coffee! We also had prepared phrases to alert the pilots to a problem without alerting the passengers. Gone were the days when passengers could go in and look at and talk to the pilots. Gone were the days when we could sit in the cockpit for a takeoff or landing. Even my mother was invited to watch the landing one time.

We also started having two air marshals onboard who were trained to protect the passengers and aircraft in case of hijackers. They introduced themselves to the crew before boarding and let us know what to do in order to alert them. We were to treat them as regular passengers, pretending we didn't know them, and if we needed to communicate, to put a small note in a magazine and say, "Sir, here is the copy you were looking for." They couldn't stand out from others, so they ordered drinks like gin & tonic or vodka & ginger ale, which we served without the alcohol but with stir sticks and lemon.

We felt like James Bond girls passing secret messages between the air marshals. They never slept but walked around a few times. They stayed with us on layovers, and at least one time I appreciated them being with us when some of the crew went to a local market in Baghdad.

I noticed a group of the locals slowly surrounding us, getting closer and closer, demanding money, and the look of the black-clad women wasn't friendly at all. Our summer dresses stood out starkly from their veiled attire. Our marshals held us close between them, and the crowd let us pass with nothing more than angry dialogue. We would have no more shopping or sightseeing that day.

We also got trained in how to disarm a bomb (seriously!) and how to detect explosives hidden on the overhead rack or inside suitcases. If we couldn't disarm the bomb, we were to surround it with blankets and pillows at the entry door, from floor to ceiling. Also we learned how to remove a gun from a terrorist. Yeah, right. In class it sounded feasible, but I'm glad I never had to find out if it would have worked in real life.

We learned some martial arts, which I was thankful for since those skills are always usable. Little me did learn to flip a big guy to the ground if he held me around the throat. Boy, do I wish I remembered how the heck I did that. A few times the captain called me to the cockpit to check on something the tower had called about—a suspicious bag or person in the cabin. This had to be done without alerting the passengers but with a glued-on smile.

Twice we were told to turn around or make a special landing because we might have a bomb onboard. Not a nice feeling, I can tell you.

Another time, we were told to prepare the cabin for an emergency landing because our landing gears would not come down. We went through the whole procedure according to the manuals but ended up with the best, soft landing ever.

A few times we had small fires in the oven or later in the film projectors. Without a word and in minutes, we'd fix the problem and had to laugh at ourselves with the extinguishers ready in our hands. The right procedures were so ingrained in our brains, we acted without even reflecting over them.

CHAPTER 27

Teheran, Iran

One time our whole crew got stuck in Teheran for ten days. One of the places in the Middle East we were flying over got involved in a war. I don't remember where or who, but this was in the midsixties. Anyway, the airways were closed for security. Somehow we were not allowed to fly around the situation, either; no airlines could. It was a mess.

At first we thought the airport would reopen after a few days and enjoyed an impromptu "vacation." Our InterContinental Hotel there was like a fairy tale setting, and they served to our rooms the biggest free breakfast I ever saw. A whole cart was filled with all kinds of fruits, croissants, brioches, toast with different marmalades, cheeses, yogurt, soft-boiled eggs, omelets, you name it. That breakfast fed me for my whole day.

Some stewardesses became friends with cousins of the Shah Reza of Persia before he was overthrown in 1979. The cousins were very much interested in beautiful stewardesses. Actually, one of the stewardesses got married there. We had a hard time trying to talk her out of it. She thought she would be treated differently than the other wives, who were cooped up in harems. She saw herself as queen of a wonderful palace. We always wondered if she ended up in a harem too.

Anyway, at that time we enjoyed the lavish dinners and tours the cousins took us to. After awhile, however, we were all kind of tired of that life and eager to get home. We had no idea how long we would be stranded in this city.

When we finally got the OK to fly out, I was reminded of Pan Am's punctuality rule. I still live with it to this day. We were all in the crew bus to get to the airport except one stewardess, who was still paying her bill at the desk. The captain looked at his watch and told the driver to go. We all told him she was coming, but his answer was that the pickup time was now. When we started to roll, we saw her coming through the doors to start toward the bus.

The driver stopped, but the captain said, "It's three minutes past pickup time. If we stop and have to load on both her and her suitcase, we will be close to ten minutes late. GO." The poor woman just stood there looking at us, a helpless expression on her face. She had to take a taxi to the airport, which was quite a distance away. And I'm sure she received a bad remark in her file.

From that day on, I was always the first on the bus and always too early for anything in my private life too, because you never know what could happen.

Teheran 1966

CHAPTER 28

Amadeus

A friend of mine in Nice, France, lost her beloved dog to a heart failure and was devastated. About four months earlier, my Cavalier King Charles spaniel female had had a litter of only two puppies. I gave away one and wanted to keep the little boy. I named him Amadeus.

The timing to give away one of my dogs was perfect, as I already had one Great Dane, two Yorkies, three Siamese cats, and the mother Cavalier. Although I wanted to keep the puppy—he was such a cutie—I didn't need another dog. I decided to surprise her with Amadeus.

I got all the paperwork from the vet and a certificate from the Kennel club, and on my next flight to Nice, away we went, him and I.

Since I worked the flight, I had to smuggle the puppy onboard or he would have been put in the cargo hole. He was too small to survive the long flight, so in he went to the good old cockpit. I did introduce him to the captain, just in case he wasn't a dog lover. He was kind enough to put a pillow and a blanket in a corner for him.

During the flight I got a call from the captain asking for a second steak dinner because a hungry dog had eaten his steak. I was lucky to have gotten a dog-loving captain.

We went through customs with no complication, and needless to say my friend didn't believe her eyes when she saw me coming with a dog.

Since dogs are allowed everywhere in France, he even went with us to a restaurant, which gave us a banquet seat so Amadeus could be more comfortable. Amadeus was able to participate in our dinner. I love Nice.

Even though I only had him a short time, he never forgot me. Every time I came to visit, he would go crazy, giving me all kinds of hugs and love.

Amadeus at 3 months

CHAPTER 29

Scuba Diving in Tahiti

Another memorable vacation in the sixties was with my mother in Tahiti.

We had our own small hut and everything was still quite primitive at that time. We enjoyed the beaches and surroundings. I loved the belly dancers every night and was in awe of the speed that they could move, even the men.

There was not much to do, since our accommodations were not a fancy big resort like you would get there now. There was, however, a small diving club with a French instructor who took guests out on tours and taught diving. Scuba diving was not yet part of hotel entertainment and not too popular among vacation guests either. It was not an activity people normally did.

But two young men were interested to learn. And so was I. Diving among the beautiful coral reefs attracted me, but as I said, this was the mid-1960s when scuba diving was a men's sport. The instructor was a little French guy with an ego twice his size who thought a woman's place was in the kitchen.

Here we go again, I thought. I was running into obstacles because I wanted to do something out of the box. I decided to enroll anyway, or perhaps in spite of the instructor. The instructor was reluctant, but I insisted, and he was going to make me regret it. He made sure from the beginning to let me know I had no business doing a man's sport, and they weren't going to help or give special care to a female because she didn't know her place. If I wanted to be involved in a man's sport, I was on my own. That really pissed me off and made me only more eager to do it, even if it killed me. I don't think I realized what I was getting into. I soon found out.

The equipment at that time was barely better than the metal cylinder with the hose attached from *20 Thousand Leagues under the Sea.* It was big and bulky and weighed more than half my own weight. From the beginning I also understood that the instructor, instead of helping me, would be making everything as difficult as possible. He had to prove a point, but so did I.

First, he made me swim approximately 650 feet back and forth in the pool, then about 350 feet while carrying the equipment.

For some reason the other two guys didn't have to prove that because he knew they were strong enough to do it. Had this happened now, I would have sued the guy for discrimination.

Then we went to the bottom of the pool to learn how to take on and off the air cylinder, to check the air gauge, to empty our masks from water, and to communicate with each other.

After that we took the boat to the ocean. The small boats they used then were regular boats, not equipped with ramps or anything to make it easier to get back up in the boat from the water as they are now. A small handheld ladder could be used if somebody in the boat would hold it. A ladder also helped because you had to grab your cylinder out of the water, which weighed you down and made it almost impossible to heave yourself up. I had to struggle with my equipment all by myself, as the instructor told the other guys not to help me. All resorts now have staff to help you with all that, but this was the beginning of scuba diving as a sport.

We stopped in about twenty-feet-deep water, where the instructor threw all my equipment to the bottom and told me to swim down, retrieve it, and put it on by myself. Meanwhile, the two guys helped each other.

On several of our outings, the instructor even came behind me and tore my mask from my face or removed my air hose. He told me it was part of the safety test to be prepared in case I got stuck on some corals. I wasn't sure I believed that. He never did that to the guys. I was so mad I forgot to panic. It's not a pleasant feeling to suddenly be without air.

Another time, he and the two other guys swam ahead of me while I was busy looking at all the beautiful corals and fish. When I looked up, I was alone—another big NO NO. You are never, ever to leave anybody alone while scuba diving; you have to be in pairs at all times. He would have been fired if he tried that now. But I didn't know that then.

We were at about forty to fifty feet deep, so the water wasn't clear and I couldn't see them ahead of me. I totally lost my bearings swimming around and then noticed that my air was very low. I saw I was about one thousand feet away from our anchored boat, alone except for maybe some sharks, out of air, and a storm brewing.

The sky by this time had turned gray and it started to rain, the waves getting higher and higher. If I panicked now, I would never make it, so I prayed to God and all my guardian angels to help me. I had a difficult time holding myself above the water with the heavy cylinder weighing me down and the waves bouncing me up and down. I used my snorkel to get some air. The smartest thing would have been to get off of the cylinder and let it go, but I would rather have drowned than heard the statement, "I told you scuba diving wasn't for females."

But it's amazing what you can do when you have to. I bobbed up and down until I reached the boat. But loading the cylinder into the boat was impossible while bobbing in the ocean. I waited until one of the waves lifted me up and then threw it in the boat.

Same for me. Inch by inch I managed to climb in.

Not a word was said when the guys came back and helped each other in. I could tell they were embarrassed and didn't even dare look at me. I think the instructor realized I wasn't going to give him the pleasure of saying the activity was not for women. He then stopped his dirty tricks and chose instead to ignore me.

We went on a deep dive, down to 350 feet, which was long and slow and boring because on the return we spent half the time hanging on a rope to decompress. At that depth, it's also too dark to see anything. But I was able to check all the boxes I needed to be certified.

Before mother and I left, although the instructor wasn't happy about it, he had no reason not to give me my certificate as a scuba diver and a diploma for deep diving, still mumbling something about how women should know their place. Since Tahiti belonged to French Polynesia, it made me one of the first women in France and maybe in all of Europe to earn that certificate.

I did several dives after that, in more civilized hotels with special boats, including staff to carry all the "lighter, more modern equipment." And in these much better-run operations, several divers were always around you in the water to check if you were OK. And someone would serve snacks and drinks and fresh towels when you came up.

I should have waited ten years to start this "manly" sport.

Civilized boat in Martinique

CHAPTER 30

Bonaire

Was it because I was born under the sign of Capricorn that I never got anything handed to me without a struggle? A flight could be half full for a whole month, but the minute I would decide to take advantage of that fact, some circumstance would happen at the last minute to fill the airplane. Another company would cancel their flight, or a mechanical problem would occur, necessitating an airplane change—to a smaller one. Or a group arrived at the last minute, or whatever to cause my family and me to be off loaded. It surprises me we still managed to make that many standby trips against all odds.

I decided to take a three-day trip with my daughter, who was thirteen years old at the time, to Bonaire, a small island in the Dutch group of the Antilles, next to Curacao, off the coast of Venezuela. This island was known for its clear water and beautiful underwater sights. I was hoping to do some scuba diving and to introduce my daughter to the beauty of the sea—at least with a snorkel first.

The trip started out fine. We arrived there without a problem, but that was too good to last. Our luggage was nowhere to be found.

Pan Am had a "fine print" that if they lost your bags, they would give you $100 to buy necessities. That amount didn't cover our new bathing suits, my camera, clothing, makeup, etc. We were told to call the small "Flamingo Airport" every day to check if they found it, which we did twice a day to make sure.

The $100 didn't cover much, but we each bought a bathing suit and cover up. Forget the pretty dresses we were going to wear for fancy dinners.

We still had a wonderful time. We walked to a nearby village to have lunch and watermelon smoothies to avoid having no suitable attire for the hotel restaurant. Except for the last night, we went early, before the other guests, and sat in an outdoor terrace and enjoyed a broiled lobster.

During the days, we spent the time mostly sunbathing, as the sun's rays did not yet have a bad reputation, and I taught my daughter to snorkel. She was amazed at what she saw underwater.

The day of departure, when we got to the airport, guess what was waiting for us? Our suitcases. Actually they had never been lost at all, but had been put in a corner of the cargo hole. Since everybody was always in a hurry getting bags out and in, nobody bothered to check properly. At least our luggage had been around the world. Since nobody thought our bags could still be onboard, nobody thought to inquire in Europe or Asia. They had been taken off and put back on again when they weren't claimed. We could tell where they'd been by all the stickers from the different countries glued to them. Remember those stickers? It was "in" to have your suitcase covered in them.

Finally back in Bonaire, an employee looked more thoroughly and found them and took the time to find a matching name.

Tell me, does this happen to you? Anyway, what really was too much was when Pan Am had the audacity to demand the $100 back since they had "never lost" the suitcases. I answered them I'd be happy to send them the toothbrushes and necessities we had to buy with it. And that was the end of it.

CHAPTER 31

An Unexpected Layover

Sometimes a big mechanical problem can turn into a wonderful unpredicted vacation.

When I was a stewardess for Pan Am, we had a trip to Paris where we stayed the whole week and made daily shuttles to Tel Aviv, Israel, three days in a row, leaving in the morning and arriving back late in the afternoon. We didn't take any luggage with us but left everything in the hotel.

The flight was difficult from the perspective of a stewardess because nearly the whole airplane was filled with passengers who required a kosher meal. That meant a special sealed box that we had to present to every kosher passenger to get their permission to open it for us so we could get the casserole out to get heated. Then, after the service, where do you store all 137 boxes? In the lavatories.

The service was also hindered by the prayer time. Passengers all gathered around the galleys to lay down their prayer mats and face east, toward the temple in Jerusalem, to have their prayer time.

On one occasion we had a mechanical problem after landing in Tel Aviv. After hanging around the airport for four and a half hours, we got sent to a hotel to spend the night. The hotel was right on the beach and we enjoyed a great dinner. We weren't allowed to drink any alcohol since we were in uniform.

Early the next day, we went to the airport, only to find that the airplane was not fixed yet. We were sent back to the hotel and told to be ready for a late departure. You would think we could have avoided getting up at the crack of dawn and slept a few more hours. But Pan Am didn't work that way.

That news still left us the whole day to take advantage of. We were not going to waste it. It was a small airplane with only four crew members and two pilots, so we knew each other well.

The hotel arranged a driver for us who spoke English well, and off we went. We drove south through the Judean desert to Masada, an ancient fortress high on a plateau overlooking the Dead Sea.

On our way back, we stopped at different places by the salt sea, also called the Dead Sea because no life can live in that much salt. It is 1,388 feet below sea level, which makes it the world's lowest place on earth. We could see the chunks and deposits of salt everywhere.

When we got back to the hotel that afternoon, we called the airport and discovered we had to wait for a part to be flown down from London. We had the whole next day off too, so we made an appointment with the driver for early the next day.

Since we had no other clothes than what we had on our backs, we had to be imaginative. The area was hot and dusty, so our clothes could definitely have used a laundering. One stewardess tied her scarf as a top, one put her blouse on backward, and one used her slip (yep, we had to wear those) as a dress with her belt. We were not going to let that problem stop us.

We were lucky to have found that driver. He was like a history book, knowledgeable of all the historic facts. So off we went to Bethlehem and Jerusalem.

In Bethlehem we saw the house where Jesus lived. Some say he was born there. In Jerusalem, we went to the West Bank, which, at that time at the end of 1960, had no wall yet between east and west. Then we walked in the old city and also up the Mount of Olives.

We felt as though we had been transported to ancient times, far from the modern world. Back in the hotel we were told the part had arrived, but it was the wrong part. That meant another day of sightseeing. Our driver was as happy as we were since we tipped him generously.

This time we drove north to the sea of Galilee and Nazareth. Of course, all around the area where Jesus walked on the sea, we were bombarded by sellers of holy water, scrolls, and other souvenirs. After a short walk around Nazareth we returned to the hotel where we said goodbye to our wonderful guide.

These three days transported us back thousands of years. All the places we visited had such an ancient vibe, a historical atmosphere, it was difficult to come back to our modern era. I will forever be grateful to have seen so much before all the wars and skirmishes destroyed so many of those areas. I will never forget this blessing of a delay.

On our way back, our flight was packed with angry passengers but a very happy crew. Shortly afterward, this flight was canceled due to unruly and unsafe conditions there.

Old Jerusalem

CHAPTER 32

High Tea at the Ritz

I happened to be home one weekend and was talking to my mother and daughter about how I loved the high tea in London. I described the pyramid dish full of cakes, pastries, and scones with clotted cream. My eight-year-old daughter thought it sounded so nice, she asked if she could come to London with me sometime. I asked my mother if she would like that also. My mother was always willing and ready to go anywhere at any moment.

I asked them both if they would like to fly to London on the next morning's flight, spend the day, drink tea at the Ritz, and come back the next day.

My daughter jumped for joy. "Yeah! Let's have tea in London!"

So we did. We left on a Saturday morning flight and arrived in time for a lovely dinner at the Ritz at Piccadilly Square. On Sunday afternoon we had one of the best high teas in London in the Palm Court at the Ritz, lavishly decorated with palm trees, ample light, and gold trim. We then hurried to catch the late flight home.

My daughter was on time for school the next day, and when asked what she did over the weekend, she answered as if it were the most normal thing to do. "We had tea in London." She couldn't understand why they all stared.

Heddy and her mother

CHAPTER 33

The Phantom of the Opera, 1986

On Pan Am flight 002, our first stop in our trip around the world was London. A couple of stewardesses asked the concierge if he could get us tickets for the popular new show *The Phantom of the Opera* by Andrew Lloyd Weber, starring his wife, Sarah Brightman, and Michael Crawford. He said it had been sold out for weeks. One of the stewardesses and I decided to take a chance there might be some unclaimed tickets, so we went to the theatre, only to find a long line of people with the same hope.

We still hung around and asked one of the hostesses if she could recommend some other show or play. We explained we were in London only for this day and were disappointed not to be able to see the *Phantom* we'd heard so much about.

She told us to wait a little longer, that she was going to find out something. We heard the show start when she came back saying, "Hurry, come with me this way." She explained that Mr. Weber had his own private lodge in case he or some friends wanted to see the show, but nobody had come today. "So here, enjoy the show," she said. There really are some nice people in the world. We had a fantastic time.

Grant you, the next morning we were rather tired, having skipped our afternoon nap on arrival and coming back late at the hotel for an early pickup, but seeing the play was well worth it.

See what a tough life we have!

CHAPTER 34

Hanky Panky

During the dinner service on a night flight to London, a woman sat alone on the right side of the first-class cabin. On the left side was a man sitting alone. The two of them started a conversation across the aisle. They both were drinking quite a bit, and by the end of the dinner, the man had moved to sit next to the woman. That is fine, but we had to monitor their heavy drinking.

When we turned off the light after dinner, we asked them to speak low in order not to bother the passengers who wanted to sleep. They obliged. In our walk-through about twenty minutes later, they appeared to have gone to sleep, covered with blankets.

Patrolling the cabin half an hour after that, I observed a suspicious bundle of blankets on the right row of seats. I slowly walked past and continued through to the back cabin, checked with the stewardess on duty, and slowly walked back up toward the front again.

This time I noticed some rustling in the bundle of blankets on the right row. I went to the front galley and asked the stewardess there to keep an eye on that row.

I started counting the liquor kits in the back cabin when I got a call from the first class. On my way close to the row we were monitoring,

I stumbled on something. I picked it up and saw it was a small ladies' underwear. I was tempted to make an announcement, asking if a lady had lost some piece of clothing. But being a good stewardess, I didn't. But I did go to the bundle and tapped gently on it, saying, "Uh, excuse me." When two heads came up, I asked politely, "Does this belong to you?" I also added that they might want to prepare for our breakfast service that was to be served shortly.

They both had returned to their original seats by breakfast time, and the funniest thing was that when they disembarked, they acted as if they didn't even know each other and went their separate ways.

Maybe they didn't remember.

CHAPTER 35

New Year's Eve

Sometimes I really have felt singled out to have had all kinds of troubles during my whole life. We Capricorns never get anything the easy way.

One New Year's Eve when most people were having fun at parties, I landed around midnight at JFK. I started my car and left our parking lot, which is located between several hangars. I drove only a half mile when my car stopped. Everything was pitch black around me. My car refused to start again.

Since this was January 1 of 1970, cell phones had not been invented yet, so here I was, in my high heels and tight skirt, walking around a bunch of deserted hangars on New Year's Eve! As luck would have it, I had only taken a couple steps when I stepped in a small hole filled with mud. There went my well-polished shoes. I did have with me my small pen light issued by Pan Am for when I walked through the dark cabin, but it wasn't strong enough to even light up my path.

I was hoping somebody was still working somewhere around all these hangars but realized the chances were slim to nil. I changed my direction to walk toward the highway instead, hoping some car would stop, but no cars were even on the road. Who would be driving around at this hour unless they were drunk and trying to get home too? When I got frozen, I went back to sit in the cold car until the next morning.

Around two a.m., I heard the sound of a motor and ran out to wave to whomever was driving at this hour. I was so desperate, I didn't consider at the time that it could have been a murderer or someone else intent on harming me. But I was lucky; it was a Pan Am employee working late. After checking my engine, he told me to wait there—as if I could go anywhere. He went back to his office to call for a tow truck. I so appreciated his help.

After half hour, I heard the wonderful sound of a tow truck. After my car was loaded up and I sat in the warm cab of the truck, the driver said everything was closed at this hour and holiday. He had nothing else to do, so he offered to drive me home and drop off the car there, and in the morning to call a repair shop who would pick it up. I gratefully accepted his offer.

Happy New Year, by the way.

CHAPTER 36

Super Blizzard in the Northeast

Between February 5 and ending February 7, 1978, a catastrophic historic nor'easter paralyzed the entire North Atlantic region for approximately a week with up to fifty-five inches of snow, taking hundreds of lives and costing millions of dollars. Even though New York wasn't the worst city affected by this super blizzard, it was enough to close all the interstates from Boston to New York, New Jersey, and Pennsylvania. I lived in the Poconos, in Pennsylvania, at that time, about 120 miles from JFK airport. We landed with a weather warning that a blizzard was coming. I left for home in a hurry, hoping to make it before it came.

It was only raining when I left New York and started on Interstate 80 to cross New Jersey to get to Pennsylvania. Twenty miles of driving later, the rain turned to sleet. Another twenty miles later, it turned to snow, and still another twenty miles after that, the snow was so thick, I couldn't see anything in front of me. Now I was in the middle of New Jersey late at night, and nobody else was crazy enough to be on the road. I fought slowly another ten miles before I came to a stop.

I dreamed of a future with portable phones, but I was totally stuck now, with the heavy snow covering my car. Though exhausted after a twenty-four-hour flight home, I kept cleaning my windows so I wouldn't be totally buried and left to die.

After about an hour I saw a lifesaver—the flashing lights of a patrol car slowly coming my way. I jumped out, waving. He asked me what I was doing there since the highway was closed at the Pennsylvania border. I explained how the snow had only been rain when I left New York and hadn't heard anything about the highways closing.

He said I wasn't far away from an exit and told me to drive in his tracks. I asked him to drive really slow and make sure he didn't lose me.

I could barely see him a few feet away, but somehow we plowed our way to a small bed and breakfast place near the exit. At least I could call home to tell my family I was OK. I spent two days there before road crews finally cleared the highway and opened it up.

After that I got a small rental apartment near the airport with four other stewardesses, in case this would happen again.

CHAPTER 37

Iced Honda

Yet another time when I got home after being away when New York had a week of below-zero temperatures, I got a shock when I saw my car in the parking lot. It was shiny and glazed like hard candy. It was beautiful—all covered in a sheet of ice. BUT, I couldn't even put my keys in the key hole to open the door. I had nothing to heat up the key, and nobody was in sight.

Again, a cell phone would have come in handy. That lot wasn't close to any buildings and was all by itself in the middle of nowhere. What else could I do then but walk around, waiting until I saw a crew member come? I expected the bus shuttle from the airport to be coming back so I could ask for help.

I waited a long time before a crew member drove in. He thankfully had a lighter and melted the ice from the door lock so I could open the door and was able to turn on the engine and heat up the car. It took another hour to defrost the window enough to get the windshield wipers to work.

I couldn't wait to get my transfer to the Atlanta base.

CHAPTER 38

Moving South

Living in Pennsylvania, I had the weather channel on the TV on all the time. I was obsessed that I wouldn't make it on time for a flight. The weather in New York could be beautiful, but in the Poconos we could have three feet of snow. My biggest problem was being able to dig myself out of the house to reach the interstate. I was out shoveling snow the minute it started in the middle of the night so it wouldn't accumulate.

Sometimes, when newscasters announced that a big storm was arriving, I went ahead and drove to a hotel near the airport in case the storm got bad. Many times it never materialized. Those years were a nightmare.

Coming home after a full day of work and having to then make the two-and-a-half-hour drive through busy New York bridges before getting to Interstate 80, I don't know how many times I caught myself falling asleep on the monotonous stretch of I-80 while crossing New Jersey between New York and Pennsylvania. One time I remember actually dreaming that I was driving. I had the radio on, the window open, I sang, and I ate, but I was still dozing off.

I went through "seasons," driving from a nice clear fall day in New York to a cloudy, rainy day in New Jersey and ending with falling snow in Pennsylvania. There were no real roads near my home in Pennsylvania at the time, sometimes just a dirt road with ditches on both sides, pitch black and risky to meet a deer face-to-face.

It's amazing I never had an accident. In hindsight, I can't believe I made that long trek for so many years. I guess you just do what you have to do.

After Delta acquired Pan Am, I talked to several Delta crew members and became convinced to move south.

I had shed my husband along the way, and by that time my daughter was engaged. There was no logical reason for me to stay in a place I hated and risk killing myself with a commute almost as long or longer than my working flight.

On a day off, I flew down to Atlanta and spent the day with a realtor. After looking at three different styles of houses, I found my dream home that was only one hour's drive to the airport on a beautiful interstate. A piece of cake. I made the move to Atlanta, Georgia, and never regretted it.

Actually, the Pan Am bankruptcy was a blessing in disguise on that point.

CHAPTER 39

Still Based in New York

I was still based in New York but lived in Atlanta, waiting for my transfer to the Atlanta base.

After almost a year of commuting between Atlanta, to New York, and back to Atlanta, that got to be too much. It was bad enough arriving from Africa, Asia, or even Europe at the most crowded hours of the day without having to hop on another flight to get home, going from one gate to another in hopes of getting on.

Leaving from Atlanta at the crack of dawn was an easier time to get to New York, but then by the time I started the long workday and night, I was already exhausted.

Therefore, I was still to be caught in another "Storm of the Century."

CHAPTER 40

The Storm of the Century

Why do I always return just in time for every blizzard in history? Couldn't I just be leaving for a change?

In March of 1993, after returning home after a week (of sunshine) flying in Africa, the captain made a big effort to be the last plane landing at JFK before the airport closed down. Thanks. We all sure wished he hadn't but had diverted to another city where we could still be on the payroll and taken care of. We also found out we had landed in the beginning of a predicted blizzard of the century. Over forty-two inches of snow fell during this March weekend.

I was still based in New York then but had moved to Atlanta, Georgia, when Delta took over Pan Am's routes. I usually hopped straight on another airplane to Atlanta. But with the airport closed, I was stuck. Another commuting flight attendant had a small apartment in Kew Gardens (called "crew" Gardens for its convenience to commuters) not far from the airport, and she invited me to stay with her. She had a car at the airport for that purpose, and we made our way to it with great difficulty.

The storm lasted the whole weekend, and all the stores were closed. We barely had anything to eat, only some stale cereal, cookies, cans of vegetables and soup, and a few eggs.

By the third day we heard over the radio (no TV) that the storm had passed and the city would start to clean up. The suburbs were another story.

We went outside to start digging out the car, armed with the only tools we could find: a small frying pan and a small Tupperware container. Since we had come from Africa, commuting from one airplane to another, all we had to wear was our uniform and regular high heels and no coats.

What we saw outside was a clean, white mountain of snow bordering the equally white sidewalk. We had to dig at regular intervals just to find the right car.

We finally found the right one and went to work. I don't have to tell you it took us the whole day with small breaks back at the apartment to warm up. I swore I would always have a box of hot cocoa powder in my apartment.

With more than three feet of snow piled up, the frying pan gave up before we were finished, the handle breaking apart. And the little Tupperware finally broke too.

This story might sound funny now, but I can assure you that at that moment, it wasn't.

Is there any doubt that I decided then and there to move to a southern base?

Delta uniform—first pants

CHAPTER 41

Pan American Airways Bankruptcy— Delta Takeover

The deregulation in 1980 of the airline industry forced Pan Am to compete with younger, more adaptable airlines. Then came the 1988 terrorist bombing of flight 103 over Lockerbie in Scotland. By 1991, Pan Am was rapidly losing money and agreed to a potentially lifesaving partnership with Delta Airlines. But Delta withheld funding at the last minute.

On December 4, 1991, Pan American World Airways collapsed. Delta Airlines acquired Pan Am and all the routes, and in one day I became unemployed and lost twenty-six years of accrued pension because of the bankruptcy.

I started preparing a resume. A few years earlier, I had already gotten certified as a real estate agent. One day I received a letter from Delta saying they were going to hire a hundred stewardesses from Pan Am with languages and skills to help them fill their new international flights, and those interested should send a resume. Delta would respond between certain dates and times.

As much as I was reluctant to start with an airline that had pulled a dirty trick on us, I couldn't see myself starting another career at my age. I answered yes, and at the said time sat by my phone, hoping

I wouldn't have to sit there for the next two weeks of enrollment. I was lucky, because at ten a.m. that first day, I got the call and a date to come in for an interview.

On said date, the interview was as nerve racking as my first interview with Pan Am decades back. It was conducted with persons, each from a different country, using their own language to question me. This time Italian was added to the list. Because I had spent six weeks in a convent/hospital in Rome with the chicken pox where nobody spoke English, I was lucky to be a fast learner and pick up enough during my stay to hold a conversation and even correspond with my caregivers by letters for several years after. The nuns were so sweet. They spoiled me and loved to hear all about flying and the world.

Once at home, I studied more, especially grammar and verbs until Pan Am officially qualified me as an Italian speaker. Delta must have been pleased with my interview because three days later I got a letter of acceptance. I was no longer a stewardess but a flight attendant. I got my wings and four small flags to pin on my uniform, representing my languages of French, Swedish, German, and Italian. A few months later I took the training for the role of "leader," which replaced the title of purser.

I qualified as a senior flight attendant, first flight attendant, A line, B line, or just A and B flight attendant. Then they set me up for their version of a round of training, all very different from my training with Pan Am. Our emergency training test was simplified to a choice of A, B, or C. And airplane charts were already printed with an empty ring on the place where we were to put the answer. We would not be required anymore to cook fresh foods or dish up peas or carve roast beef—or carry all the serving tools. We still had quite a quantity of manuals, though.

We learned to reheat casseroles for coach and serve precooked first-class entrees. No need for serving with spoon and forks, just a big spoon or tongs. No more cheese trays to be cut.

The old Pan Am rules might have been exaggerated, but when Delta took over, they went way too much the other way. The strict way of life was now more relaxed.

To be grounded by Pan Am if we gained one pound was crazy, but I didn't agree that the airlines had to allow any flight attendant to gain twenty or thirty pounds without penalty, for fear of her cry of discrimination. I believed an airline should have the right to choose how they wanted their flight attendants to look. In addition, on a more practical level, I can tell you from experience that it is impossible to cross over to the other side of a smaller airplane if the only passageway is blocked by a 160-pound flight attendant. Not even sideways can you get past. I also wonder how it would be possible for her to fit through the escape hatch. And I personally don't think huge colored plastic earrings are very professional.

The introduction of male flight attendants made for a whole different atmosphere too. Our uniform got more relaxed, too. For the first time we could wear pants, and heels as low as two inches. And we were allowed any choice of hairdo or makeup. And I could even remove my jacket if I got hot.

Some changes were definitely an improvement.

CHAPTER 42

911

I was lucky to land home the night before September 11, 2001. When I turned on the TV the next morning, I could not believe my eyes.

When I first saw the plane heading straight for the World Trade Center in New York, I thought the pilot must have lost control of the plane. I was sure he was going to turn anytime. Then I realized, my God, he's going to hit the tower. I heard the Pentagon had been hit also.

I stayed glued the whole day to the TV, not believing such a thing could happen. What a horrible day.

Then I received a call that all my flights were canceled until further notice. Later I heard all airports in America were closed and all travelers stranded everywhere, with nowhere to go because within a short time all hotels around the airports were full.

I called briefing to ask if I could be of help at the airport in taking care of the stranded passengers. They accepted immediately, and off I went to pass sandwiches, beverages, blankets, pillows, and whatever I could help with.

A couple of days later I got assigned the first flight to Rome, leaving with a minimum crew since many of them were stuck abroad. All incoming flights had also been canceled since all airways over the US were closed. The few departures were thoroughly checked. On our arrival in Rome, we were surrounded by armed soldiers with rifles and escorted to our crew bus, which made us feel like criminals.

On the return flight, again the military came with us to the airplane with K9 dogs trained to sniff for explosives while the crew waited on the ramp. I've always felt safe after the dogs checked the aircraft. They could smell things that no human could see, and never missed a place. This checking went on for several months.

One time, again in Rome, waiting on the ramp for the K9, this big German shepherd walked off the aircraft and straight to my open tote bag. He dove in it and grabbed the prosciutto sandwich I had bought in the airport, paper bag and all. Within minutes it was gone. I was still in shock, and all the military and crew laughed—except me, who had lost my lunch. Don't they feed those dogs?

CHAPTER 43

Italian Prosciutto

That last story reminded me of another flight to Rome, long before 911. I did say I loved Italy, but did I mention how I loved the "real Italian" prosciutto? This one you cannot buy in the States because of a law that requires all meat products to be cooked to a certain temperature. Prosciutto is not cooked, only cured. I had bought half a kilo (about two pounds) of the cured meat to take home to my family, even though it was a big no no.

I wrapped it tight in plastic wrap, then foil, then heavy paper, and rolled it in my nightgown in my suitcase so the agriculture doggie in New York customs would not be able to smell it. Since I am usually an honest person, I was sick the entire flight home with the thought I could be caught smuggling.

I wasn't, though. I got home and set a festive table for the occasion.

At that time I owned a Great Dane who stood six feet tall. I prepared a big serving dish with the prosciutto in the middle of the table and went to get a crusty baguette from the oven. When I came back to the dining room, my dog saw me and sat down with a totally innocent look, like dogs have when they are guilty.

My heart stopped and a NO! came out of me. A third of my precious, expensive prosciutto was gone. My first thought was to kill the thief, but we all had to laugh, because the moral of the story is that one way or another, you do get punished for breaking the law.

The one who ate the prosciutto

CHAPTER 44

More Places

I went to many more places, but nothing to make a big story of, even though they all had something memorable. But in my exciting life, I:

- Sat through a whole bullfight with the number-one bullfighter, El Cordobés, in Barcelona; the crowd went wild

- Saw the world's fastest tap dancer, José Greco, and his band in Madrid, Spain

- Saw the opera *Aida* in Rome's Terme di Caracalla, with live elephants, giraffes, camels, horses, and hundreds of participants; unforgettable! I enjoyed more opera at La Scala di Milano.

- Heard my favorite tenor, Jussi Björling, in a couple of operas in Stockholm, Sweden; I also heard a Mozart concert inside his house in Salzburg, Austria

- Saw the famous Lipizzaner stallions in Vienna, Austria

- Walked around the Acropolis and more in Athens, Greece; I also saw The Vatican, the Colosseum, and just about all the churches in Rome, Italy; I went under the Bridge of Sighs in a gondola and fed the pigeons of the Piazzo San Marco in Venice, Italy

- Visited the hand-blown glass factory in Murano, the grotto d'Azura in Capri, the volcanoes Solfatara, Vesuvius, Pompeii, and Etna in Sicily
- Toured the pyramids in Cairo, Egypt; picture mother and me, each on top of a camel in skirt and heels; these were the times when a lady did not wear pants
- Walked around the souks of Damascus and Baghdad
- Drove through Baalbeck, Byblos, and Beirut—all cities in Lebanon—and loved seeing what is left of their famous cedar forests
- Saw rice plantations and the Great Wall of China
- Saw Victoria Falls, Chania Falls, and more beautiful ones I don't know the names of in Africa; and I saw Niagara Falls closer to home
- Drove up the coast of the "Cote d' Azure" from Cannes, Nice, Monaco, and Monte Carlo up and down narrow curving roads—so scary, but oh so beautiful with the blue Mediterranean below—all the way to Italy
- Other highlights:
- Windmills and tulips as far as the eye could see in Holland
- Boat tour on the waterway that wound through the town and under the bridges of Bruges, Belgium
- Crossing from West Berlin to East Berlin in Germany at Checkpoint Charlie, a symbol of the Cold War, when it was still in operation

- Wonderful dinner as it was served in the 1600s with music and dress from that time in Bunratty Castle in Ireland
- The little mermaid in Copenhagen, Denmark
- Up north in Sweden, an ice bar in an ice hotel; yes, absolutely everything was made of ice, including the walls, furniture, and drinking glasses; I also saw the incredible aurora borealis
- The Alps, which I flew over on a perfectly clear day, and I felt like I was so close I could touch those snowy peaks
- Glaciers in Alaska; the weather was so cold, Pan Am issued the crew big, furry parkas on arrival (to be returned)
- Versailles, Fontainebleau, and most well-known castles, churches, and cathedrals, as well as nearly every museum in Europe
- Most every tropical island in the Bahamas and Hawaii
- "Christ the Redeemer" statue on top of the mountain overlooking Rio de Janeiro, sunning on Copacabana beach—our hotel only a few feet from the beach—and also Buenos Aires and Sao Paulo
- Johannesburg, South Africa, where I bought a big real ostrich egg that I was so afraid of breaking on the long way home; I still have it
- Closer to home, all the narrow spiral stairs inside the arm of the Statue of Liberty in New York City, which I climbed all the way up to the flame and walked around it before that section was closed to tourists

Some of the places I got to visit you cannot go to now, including the Blue Mosque in Istanbul, Turkey; the city of Baghdad, Iraq;

and the huge souk (market) in Damascus, Syria, all separated into sections selling different types of items. I remember the big area with hundreds of all colors of pieces of dyed fabric. Another spot had hundreds of copper items—all worked with inlays of silver and mother of pearl—and also a big gold market.

I'm sure I forgot some places I visited, but two I never got to see are Australia and New Zealand. Pan Am flew there from their Hawaii base, and I would have needed an extra-long vacation to take a trip that far. That is one of my few regrets.

The Alps 1989

Cairo with Mother 1967

Blue Mosque in Istanbul, Turkey

Acropolis, Athens

Hong Kong 1976 — Mother and Alexandra

Hong Kong 1976

On my previous trip, I'd told the immigration guys my mother would be coming for her very first time to the United States on my next flight. They duly made a note, and there was an officer waiting for her at the foot of the airplane's stairs! He treated my mother like a true VIP and signed all her papers there and then—can you imagine that happening nowadays?

Sitting on the engine

Epilogue

I retired at seventy-five years old, not because I couldn't handle the jet lag or the hard work on the airplane anymore, but because the glamour was gone. It had become more like a job getting hundreds of traveling strangers from point A to point B. Our layover time got shorter and shorter the more frequent the flights became. It finally went to the minimum of eight hours, barely enough time to get some sleep.

Also, when the airlines cut down on comfort and food, the passengers initially responded with bad moods. They then directed all their resentment to the face of the airline, which was us, the flight crew.

For the passengers, flying isn't special anymore either. It is only a means of transportation to reach a destination as fast as possible, while in the beginning, air travel was a luxury and a major part of any vacation. Passengers used to come onboard all dressed up as if they were visiting a fancy restaurant or enjoying an evening out. They were excited, came with big expectations, and got excellent service. They were pampered, spoiled with gifts, and treated as royalty. The food, catered from Maxim's in Paris, was five stars.

Gone is the excitement of flying. Gone are the little white gloves, replaced by plastic ones to pick up trash and deposit it straight in a big bag, also plastic, instead of how we used to collect it with a small silver tray. Ouch.

My life was actually timed perfectly. Flying in the beginning years of air travel can never be duplicated, even if it was quite a demanding career. I got to experience a world that does not exist anymore. I lived in an era that is gone, and I'm not sure I like the new one better. Even with all the modern inventions I could have used in my time (yes, I really would have enjoyed a phone), I am so glad I started when commercial flying was brand new and special, the good old times, the glamour years, the golden age of flying.

Even the modern perks like free passes are only useful if you have time to waste several hours or sometimes days at an airport trying to get a seat, as most flights are full now. And that waiting game happens after spending time going through security lines to get checked, having to practically get naked to satisfy security personnel. (It must be a small revenge for the times we were in uniform and just sped through.)

But even though I long for those bygone glamourous years, I'm grateful to Pan Am for giving me the opportunity to have had such an exciting career—unusual for a woman at that time. I learned, I grew in confidence, and I experienced more sights and smells than I can even recall.

And, you might wonder if I ever said some of those cheeky comments out loud, the ones where I tell the passengers exactly how it is: "No, I'm too busy to get you another drink" or "Please sit down; now is *not* a good time to go to the bathroom." I didn't. I remained a professional to the end.

I'm proud to be one of the original Pan Am stewardesses, the golden girls of the air.

Made in United States
North Haven, CT
09 January 2025

64205526R00085